Zeev Gilkis

Unlock Bliss:
A Memoir Of Getting Happier

Zeev Gilkis
Unlock Bliss

© All Rights Reserved to Zeev Gilkis (2019)

Editing: Dalia Talmon
Illustrations: Omri Gilkis
Graphic Editor: Studio Rubin

No part of this publication may be reproduced or transmitted in any form or by any means, electronic or mechanical, including photocopy, recording, Internet web storage or any information storage and retrieval system without explicit
permission in writing from the author.

ISBN-13: 978-9655750188

Contact: zgilkis@gmail.com

I would like to thank my dear family and friends, who read and commented on the early versions of this book. Your feedback and comments helped me a lot and contributed to the final version of this book.

Thanks!

 **Zeev Gilkis**, PhD, was the founder of AMIT, an institute for bio-medical development at Technion. For more than eight years he was the CEO of the institute and led the establishment of five start-ups in various fields of medicine, serving as the chairman of the Board of Directors on all five.

For over 11 years he held senior management positions at Comverse Technology (Nasdaq CNSI).

He earned his PhD with a thesis on Artificial Intelligence, and in addition, holds graduate degrees in mathematics, statistics and computer science and MSc in mathematics.

Gilkis served in the mythological 8200 SIGINT Unit of the Israeli Intelligence for 17 years, and was awarded the highest "Award for Israeli National Security" projects by the President of Israel.

He served as the first Israeli military attaché to Poland and Hungary.

In addition to his diversified career, he has devoted most of his free time to neuro-science, health and nutrition.

He is a vegan, practices yoga and meditation.

 All the illustrations in this book were created by **Omri Gilkis**.

Omri Gilkis is an architect, illustrator, storyboard writer, 3D modeler and a concept artist.

Although the motive for living a happier life lies at the core of this book, and there is logic in the order of the chapters, each chapter is self-contained, so it is possible to read this book in any chapter order one chooses.

List of contents:

Chapter 1 - **About the book**. 9

Chapter 2 - **My story**. 11

Chapter 3 - **The decision to write** 17

Chapter 4 – **The tale of "big stones"**. 21

Chapter 5 – **Happiness** 25

Chapter 6 – **Moments of joy and elation** 36

Chapter 7 – **From pleasure to addiction and about money and happiness** 41

Chapter 8 – **Coordinating expectations** 46

Chapter 9 – **Sub-consciousness and intuition** 52

Chapter 10 – **Making Decisions** 61

Chapter 11 – **How I got rid of headaches** 78

Chapter 12 – **Nutrition and Health** 89

Chapter 13 – **An Interlude** 103

Chapter 14 – **Family** 105

Chapter 15 – **People** 115

Chapter 16 – **Career and Profession** 125

Chapter 17 – **Success and luck** 129

Chapter 18 – **Physical activity** 134

Chapter 19 – **Meditation** 143

Chapter 20 – **"Stop Worrying and Start Living"** ... 150

Chapter 21 – **Learning** 155

Chapter 22 – **Between her and him** 165

Chapter 23 - **A short love story** 172

Chapter 24 - **Getting older: Dreams, wishes, aspirations and "The Bucket List"** 174

Chapter 25 – **Time, and reversing aging** 180

Chapter 26 - **About me** 192

Chapter 27 - **Coda** 196

Chapter 1 - About the book

This book is about happiness, those aspects of life relevant to being happy, some relevant processes in the brain and personal examples from my life experience.

There are many books about happiness. Most of them are interesting and enjoyable. Some are more philosophical, some less, and some leave us with important questions unanswered.

"Can we live a happier life?!" is a practical book. It deals with many aspects of happiness, some of which do not seem related at first glance.

There is no definite standard to evaluate happiness, or "how well is my life going". In many cultures it is common to view wealth as a measure of one's success, and maybe even of happiness. However, studies have clearly shown that wealth, beyond some satisfying level, is no guarantee for more happiness.

In this book I propose a new index – **HQ**, like IQ and EQ, as a measuring yardstick to one's potential to feel happy.

The book is based on my personal observations and introspections, which began 38 years ago when I started to meditate. The process intensified when I was diagnosed with colorectal cancer, receiving the highest priority and thought since then.

Each chapter includes some practical advice which can be easily applied in daily life.

Reaching out for such a book requires a level of openness, curiosity and self-searching, so reading these words means that you are on the right path. Congratulations!

Chapter 2 - My story

Some 14 years ago I was diagnosed with colorectal cancer, stage three out of four, which had probably been developing for years.

The symptoms were there, but when one doesn't allow himself to imagine such a possibility, he disregards the signs.

Suddenly, my self-image changed dramatically, from a healthy person to one having an advanced stage cancer.

The odds did not look good; my father and both of my mother's brothers died of cancer. All three stories were quite tragic, which was more or less all I knew then about the disease.

Once I accepted my new status, "I have cancer", I moved on to the action mode (see Chapter 20. "Stop Worrying and Start Living", the life philosophy of Dale Carnegie, later in the book).

I began studying books and the Internet intensively, and went for numerous consultations.

I decided to undergo neo-adjuvant therapy – a combination of radiation and chemotherapy (yes, both chemotherapy and radiation, simultaneously). This is a preparatory regime which is meant to increase the odds of successful surgery. Chemotherapy mainly attacks fast-dividing cells, a property of cancerous cells. But there are also healthy cells which divide quickly, and harming them, causes unpleasant side effects.

Radiation therapy is a local treatment directed at the cancerous area. When it reaches the cancerous cells, it destroys many of them or impedes their further advancement. However "on the way" it also traverses through healthy tissues and may damage them as well, leading to more side effects.

After these two preparatory processes, the probability of successful surgery is much higher.

Decisions were made, there was a plan.

Before beginning chemotherapy and all this "CRBN" war (Chemical, Radiological, Biological and Nuclear) against "that thing" deep inside my body, I went to Hararit [a mountain community in Galilee, its residents engaged in transcendental meditation] for a few days, to be alone with my thoughts.

It is good to be alone with our thoughts from time to time, although I don't wish anybody such circumstances. Since the Siddhis Course (a type of advanced meditation, see the Meditation Chapter, 19), I grew to love this place which is my favorite to introspect, reflect, meditate and think about life.

I took notes of my thoughts about life and death and the meaning of life. Recently, when I browsed through these notes, I was surprised at how morbid they sounded. I couldn't free myself from thoughts of my funeral.

I realized that we are all here on borrowed time and no one lives forever. The cancer caused me to realize how finite life is. My thoughts were morbid, but at the time I had no idea how all this will end. For my father and uncles there was no happy end.

In addition, the statistics were against me. Currently the probability of surviving a colorectal cancer stage three is around 40%, but at the time it was only 30%.

I returned from Hararit stronger, determined to face the cancer and to fight it! I'm not going to surrender, I'm declaring war! But not just a "conventional war" (although the radiations and chemotherapy weren't exactly a conventional war either).

In addition, I underwent all available alternative medical treatments: Chinese medicine, thermotherapy and even sound therapy.

Thermotherapy or hyperthermia is a type of cancer treatment in which body tissues are exposed to high temperatures created by focused radio-waves. Research has shown that high temperatures can damage and kill cancer cells. Concurrently some cooling is applied to the skin in order to prevent burns. This therapy is usually less harmful to normal tissues.

A good friend introduced me to two researchers who had found that in animal trials on rats, amaranth showed a very strong anti-cancer therapeutic effect. At that time amaranth wasn't available in Israel, so I had to order it from Prague. Unfortunately the supplier stopped responding after a severe flooding there.

These were difficult times for me. The chemotherapy was disgusting and both chemotherapy and the radiation caused unpleasant side effects.

I received the chemo through a port-a-cath, which was implanted under the skin, on the right side of my chest - a convenient "site" where it doesn't interfere with anything important. On the internal side, the catheter connects the port to a vein. On the external side, a tubule attaches to a larger container, containing "the drink" – the chemo-drug.

Under the skin, the port has a septum through which drugs can be injected and blood samples can be drawn numerous times. This smethod provides less discomfort than the more typical "needle stick".

There are several advantages to the aforementioned method: the drug (poison?!) flows slowly and uniformly throughout the day and night, as opposed to a daily or weekly dosage which have to be much higher. In this way it's much easier for the body to "live with it" and fewer side effects are caused. Also the external container can be conveniently attached to the belt, enabling walking around without constraints.

In times like that, new thoughts suddenly appear, about the life before, the possibilities "after", appreciating what we have and swearing that "if I survive I will...."

Indeed I made some important promises to myself. I began to understand what is more important and what is less so.

The roots of many of the understandings presented later in this book commenced at that time.

It is hard to appreciate happiness, when everything is going well, at least on the external level. In such a time we dive deeper into our mind and soul.

After finishing the "preparatory stage" – chemotherapy and radiation – came surgery.

The operation was quite long, lasting for many hours. Biopsies were taken and sent out for pathology, in order to confirm clear margins. Clear margins mean that the tumor has been removed and that it is surrounded by a rim of healthy tissue free of cancer cells. This process ensures that the likelihood of a residue of cancer cells is low.

The surgery was successful!

Following the operation, I underwent another series of chemotherapy, this time prophylactic, just in case any cancerous cells survived somewhere in my body.

Since then I go for a yearly checkup, which appears to be OK.

Maybe the crazy pace of life I was living in: Highest priority given to work and career, trying to achieve as much as possible (and beyond...) and a lower priority given to a healthy lifestyle, the cancer was the warning I needed. However it was quite an expensive message.

These were nine months of struggle, ups and downs, one day optimistic and another day pessimistic, not knowing how it will end.

These extremely intensive times are forever imprinted on my mind and have had a major influence on my approach to life: Always seeing the half-full glass, better understanding of what really counts in life and my attitude towards everything.

All these understandings, which began then and have developed during the years through self-search, introspection, studying and thinking, have led to many conclusions about various aspects of life.

I am happy to share these understandings, conclusions and practical solutions throughout this book.

Today I am healthy and happy, probably much happier than I was before and eventually found the time to write this book.

Chapter 3 - The decision to write

Once I attended a lecture about happiness.

The lecturer talked about how a happy person can become even happier.

Someone from the audience asked: "what will he do with so much happiness?"

The answer also came from the audience: "In Cabbala there is a saying that the happier a person is, the more he or she wants to share with others".

Since my recovery from cancer thirteen years ago, I am healthy and happy, even happier than before, and have decided that now it's my duty to share.

Throughout the years I have shared all which I have learned with others, the understandings of life as well as some original ideas. At first it was mainly with my family and a few close friends. Later, it was with my coworkers and employees, many of whom became friends.

The warm feedback encouraged me to also share with strangers. Their reaction strengthened even more my decision to share with those who might be interested.

Below is a nice example.

In October 2013, I was invited to give a few lectures in Taiwan. The hosts arranged a guide to show me around between the formal lectures and meetings. After the visit I received a touching email from her. Here is a short citation:

> *"There is an old saying in Chinese* 與人為善,
> *means that bring out the best in people,*
> *hopefully someday I can be as* 與人為善 *as you are."*

What could be a better way to share than to write a book?

I have included a few quotations from some wise well-known and respected people. These citations support many of my claims, which actually aren't only mine...

The opening chapters of this book are about happiness, which is the key motif. It continues with a mathematical formula for bursts of happiness and joy, chapters about other aspects of life such as coordinating expectations, pleasures and addictions, family, health and nutrition, making decisions and more; as all these aspects of life are relevant to being happy and being happy influences all of them.

To be practical and to demonstrate the concepts, I have included many examples, some from my personal experience, a few well-known stories, and two "synthetic" mini-stories in the chapter about happiness.

To make the reading experience more pleasurable, I asked my gifted son Omri, to enrich some of the stories and examples with his lovely illustrations, and added photos for the same purpose.

I believe that the illustrations are an art by themselves, and hope that you will enjoy them, as much as I do.

Once we finish reading a book, we are usually left with some key ideas, yet forget many of the details. Enjoying the illustrations should help remember the concepts associated with them. After all, we are very vision-oriented creatures; as the saying goes: "A picture is worth a thousand words".

Ten years ago, I was offered to submit my candidacy for establishing and heading an institute of bio-medical development at Technion.

My first reaction was: "Me?! But I'm a mathematician!"

Yet, at the same moment I realized that this could be an opportunity to make my (hidden) dream come true. The next day I submitted my CV, being ready to take the risk and give up the attractive position of Investments' Manager at Comverse Technology, which was quite a successful company at that time.

Following quite a lengthy process, I was chosen and nominated as the CEO of the Institute, which I established and have managed quite successfully since then, for more than eight years.

When I decided to write this book, despite the urge to write, I asked myself: "Me?! a book?? But I'm a mathematician!"

Then, another mathematician came to my mind: The great Charles Lutwidge Dodgson, better known by his pen name, **Lewis Carroll**.

I have no pretensions of reaching the heights of Lewis Carroll, neither as a writer nor as a mathematician, but his phenomenal success has proven that mathematicians can write books.

Chapter 4 – The tale of "big stones"

I decided to open with a well-known story, assuming that even those who have heard it, do not necessarily apply it in their daily life. We often hear wise truths, but give up on the effort of implementing them in our daily life.

So here is the story; reading it will take about three minutes, but it is worth devoting another five to dwell on it.

One day a savvy teacher was invited to speak to a group of very successful managers about managing time.
He looked at the managers and said: "we are going to do an experiment".
He pulled out a very large glass jar and set it on the table in front of him. Then he took out about a dozen big stones and placed them, one by one, into the jar.
When the jar was full and no more stones could fit inside, he asked, "Is this jar full?"
Everyone answered, "Yes."
"Are you sure?" he asked. "Let's see." He reached under the table, pulled out some gravel and dumped it in. He shook the jar, causing the gravel to work itself down into the crevices

between the big stones. Then he asked the audience again, "Is the jar full?"

The audience was catching on quickly. "Probably not," one of them answered.

"Right!" he replied. He then brought out a bucket of sand. He started pouring the sand into the spaces between the stones and the gravel. When he was finished he asked again, "Is this jar full?"

This time everybody shouted "No".

"Correct!" he replied. Then he grabbed a pitcher of water and poured it in until the jar was full to the brim. The managers looked at the full jar, then looked back at the old lecturer.

The lecturer looked back at the audience and asked: "What is the big truth we can learn from this experiment?"

One of the managers responded, *"no matter how full your schedule is, if you really try hard, you can always fit some more things into it!"*

The teacher said "That's probably true, but this is not the main point", he said.

"The big truth is, that if you don't put the big stones in first, you will never get them in at all."

The room grew silent as everyone contemplated the meaning of these wise words.

The old teacher looked again at the audience and asked: "What are the big stones in your life? Family? Relationships? Health? Spirituality? Fulfilling your dreams? To do what you really love to do?

The first thing is to identify what is most important and valuable to us.

Without getting your big stones in place first, they will never ever get in. You can be busy playing around with the gravel, sand and water in your life (the peripheral, miscellaneous and day-to-day activities) and your "big stones" will always be left out, with no room for them in your life.

Are you working to get the big stones in place? Or have you neglected them?

If we do not consciously attend to our big stones, we will never get to them. Don't push them to a 'later' or 'next time'. The big stones do not fall into place by themselves. There will always be room in our life for the gravel, sand and water, no matter when or where. But for there to be room to place our big stones, we need to deliberately make the decision to put them in first.

Start to consciously take action and get your big stones in. Only then you will start to gain the big payoffs and rewards you wish for in your life.

Chapter 5 – Happiness

Happiness is mostly a subjective feeling. It is a mental or emotional state of well-being, defined by positive or pleasant emotions.

In the book "The How of Happiness", the author, Sonja Lyubomirsky, concludes that, based on a study on twins, one's happiness level is about 50% determined by genetics (the happiness "set point"). Only 10% is affected by life circumstances and situations. The remaining 40% is determined by habits, behaviors and thought patterns which we can address directly, using intentional actions. This part is determined by us, by our mind and mental attitude. The way we consciously or subconsciously, "decide" to see ourselves: happy, less happy or miserable.

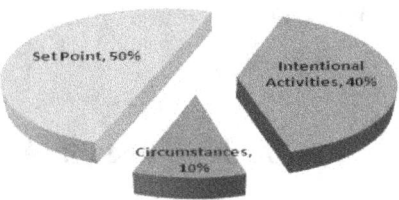

What Determines Happiness?

> Happiness Quotient - HQ, similarly to IQ and EQ, is a measuring scale of one's potential for feeling happy.

Why is it important to measure one's potential to be happy?

Because we can learn from any feedback, and we are affected by any question that turns our attention to various aspects of life, which we usually take for granted.

The list of factors influencing our HQ and their relevant "weights" was compiled based on a pilot study. The list includes aspects of life such as different family relationships, health and career which are commonly perceived as the "basis for happiness", and others, less obvious.

The key point of HQ is to measure us on a "scale", in comparison with others.

Comparing ourselves to others is natural and instinctive, as we are very social beings. We compare ourselves to our classmates in school, in college, in the work place, how many friends we have on Facebook and actually in almost everything.

So why not compare ourselves to others in happiness?

Maybe, if we become aware that our standing is quite good in many aspects (even if not in all of them), we will be more appreciative of what we do have, and feel happier?!

As above said, a large part of how happy we feel, about 40%, is determined by us, in our brain, our mind.

It is reasonable to assume that many people, maybe most of us, do not ponder on a daily basis about what they have: family, children, health etc. The process of answering the relevant questions, the score and some additional feedback, shall bring all these aspects to our attention, and serve as a good background and reference for our feeling of being happy, by influencing "the other 40%".

More than seven billion people inhabit our planet. If you have decided to purchase this book, it says something about your self-awareness. It also means that you can read and can afford to buy a book. This automatically places you in the top 10% of the world's population, in many aspects of life. But not necessarily in the top 10% on the scale of how happy you are.

Filling out the HQ questionnaire at the www.HQ100.co.il website, will not only provide you with the score of your happiness potential, but will also bring to your attention some of the important aspects of life, relevant to being happy.

In the following chapters of this book, these diverse aspects will be addressed together with analyses, examples and practical ideas which can easily be implemented.

Just as a reminder, we are addressing the *potential* of being happy, not necessarily how happy you are right now.

If you want to test your current level of happiness, there is a nice website - happiness-survey.com, which uses a questionnaire developed at Oxford University.

It might be interesting to take such a test before reading this book and again, after the reading.

To demonstrate the idea of HQ, here are three short stories:

Story No. 1

John travels to Cuba to see how people live on that poor island.

The average monthly salary in Cuba rose in 2013 by 1% to 470 peso, i.e. ~$20.

John was curious how people could live on less than a dollar a day.

While having a drink in a bistro he asked Oryana, a beautiful waitress, to come dance with him. "Sure", she replied "please come and join me and my friends at the Zorba Club tonight."

John went to "Zorba" and met Oryana and her friends, Fidel, Miguel, Maria and Francesca. All ordered Margaritas and, after enjoying the drink, began dancing. They exchanged dancing partners so John danced with Oryana, Francesca and Maria.

The evening went very well and the Cubans looked relaxed and wholly devoted to their dancing, as if their tough life outside did not exist. They looked happy.

During one of the breaks John asked Oryana how much she earns. Her answer was – "300 peso per month."

"So how do you manage?" John asked.

"Well, I like simple food, such as rice, which is very cheap, and I know many recipes. Besides, it is very healthy not to eat too much. My clothes are made here in Cuba, so they are

very cheap. All in all I manage quite well. I have a brother and a sister, whom I love very much and when I come home, our dog Ringo welcomes me with lots of love. I'm happy!"

Oryana would get a high HQ.

Story No. 2

A Chinese millionaire comes for a visit to Israel

A Chinese millionaire came for a visit to Israel. In a crowded restaurant on the Tel Aviv beach, he saw a young couple deep in discussion. They looked quite happy.

In a country which has known so many wars, and where rockets could fall anywhere, he expected to see worried faces.

He approached the couple and asked whether he could join them, offering to invite them for dinner and in return learn about their life in Israel.

"Sure!" replied the young fellow. "We'd be happy to tell you about life here. As for dinner, thanks for the invite but we have already eaten."

"So, how do you live here, while rockets might fall even on Tel Aviv?" he asked.

"Well, we became used to it." the girl replied. "And now that we have the 'Iron Dome' (a missile interception system developed by RAFAEL – an Israeli defense industry company) to protect us, the danger of casualties is low", the man added.

"Do you have children?" asked the Chinese. "Sure, three. This is the average number in Israel. They are wonderful! And what about you?"

"Well, I have one son. As you know, there are restrictions in China. But I don't see him often, I prefer not to talk about it."

"Oh, we are sorry." said the young man quietly.

"Well, I have a good business - 250 employees - though I work 12 hours a day, no vacation. This is the first time I have taken a vacation in three years."

The Chinese millionaire would probably get a low HQ.

Story No. 3

The happy man's shirt

There once was a kingdom ruled by a very good king whom everybody loved. One day, the king became severely ill and fell into a deep depression. Nothing could make him smile. The best doctors of the kingdom failed to cure him.

Eventually an old sage offered a cure: Find a really happy man and bring his shirt to the king. Once the king wears the happy man's shirt he will be cured and happy again.

Heralds were sent around the country to ask everyone how happy they are. They first approached wealthy men, then wise men, clergymen and army generals, but all admitted that actually they were not that happy.

The ministers were desperate, they couldn't save the king.

Suddenly one of the messengers heard happy singing coming out from a small depleted hut in the forest. He knocked on the door, then, when nobody answered he slowly opened it. What he saw was a very poorly dressed family, singing, laughing and dancing. The messenger asked the old man who seemed to be the head of the family: "Dear man, are you happy?"

"Sure I'm happy" replied the poor man. "I have my loving family. We have our hut, which is good enough for us, and we love to sing and dance. What else does a man need in order to be happy?!"

"Dear man", said the messenger, "Can you give me your shirt for the king? In return you can ask for whatever you want."

The man laughed; "I would be happy to give the king my shirt, but I have only these tattered clothes which you see on me, I have no shirt!"

Summary

In my approach to life, I try to see the positive side of everything. With some perspective, we can almost always find a positive side to any event or circumstance.

When I was looking for validation of my approach, I came across a nice quote of Charles Dickens:

> "Reflect on your present blessings of which every man has many, but not on your past misfortunes, of which all men have some."

The happiest people don't have the best of everything, they just make the best of everything.

The Long and Winding Road to Happiness

The process is a slow evolution; we can't change our habits in one day.

According to a study[1], changing habits takes from three weeks up to six months. On average it takes about two months.

But once we decide and persist, everything is possible.

The key thoughts of this chapter:

✓ Happiness is a subjective feeling.

✓ Happiness is potentially in our mind and it is possible to be happy, even in a situation which looks bad.

✓ To be happy is a choice.

✓ *"Who is rich? He that rejoices in his portion."* Benjamin Franklin

✓ *"Happiness consists more in the small pleasures that occur every day, than in great pieces of good fortune that happen but seldom to a man in the course of his life."* Benjamin Franklin

---

(1) "How are habits formed: Modelling habit formation in the real world". Phillippa Lally and her team: Cornelia H. M. van Jaarsveld, Henry W. W. Potts and Jane Wardle. The European Journal of Social Psychology volume 40, October 2010

Chapter 6 – Moments of joy and elation

Happiness is usually a lasting feeling, a state of mind, being with us most of the time. One can call it a "strategic" state of mind.

But in addition, certain (good) situations award us moments of pleasant joy, elation or even short bliss. As opposed to being on a "strategic level", these moments are on a "tactic level".

For example, winning the lottery would definitely bring such a moment of great joy, however not necessarily one that lasts long. Researches show that more money, beyond some satisfactory level, doesn't necessarily bring more happiness.

As a mathematician, I'm proposing a mathematical formula for joy:

$$J = T/S$$

J = joy

T = time of expectation

S = how sudden the happy event occurs

This formula means that the longer we were expecting something to happen, the more joy we will feel when it occurs.

And the more sudden the event is, the happier we'll be at that moment. Thus, we can create happy moments, and

one of the means is the effect of surprise, especially for others.

We have successfully used this formula many times for our children. For example, when we bought a fish aquarium for our youngest son Omri. We put it in his room at night, while he was asleep (not an easy task). When he opened his eyes in the morning he was obviously very happy.

Another example is, when we find something we have been looking for, for a long time.

Below are two nice examples from my personal experience.

During the Yom Kippur War (October 1973), I served as a

soldier in the Sinai desert. Our post was on Daphna, a small island, in the Bardawille Bay. Our mission there was to guard a small but important navy base.

The only way out of the island was by a boat, a yellow boat.

By the end of October the war was over, yet we had to stay there for another few months, until the ceasefire talks were concluded.

Eventually, at the end of February, we were notified that we are to be released soon, as we were a university students' unit and not a full service military one. We have been staying there for three months, so the first condition for a burst of joy was fulfilled.

Yet, for some reason time passed and the yellow boat did not arrive.

Quite frustrating.

Then, suddenly a big helicopter appeared, which, as we were told, came for us!

Now the second condition, that of the suddenness of the event, was fulfilled too, and we were all very happy.

All that happened on March 1st 1974, my 23rd birthday. My colleagues directed all their joyfulness at me – lifting me up (literally) in the air 24 times. We were young, and in good physical condition.

Another example, quite different, was my driver's license test. I had to park backwards uphill. It was a challenging exercise and I failed. I assumed I failed the test. So when I got the call telling me I passed, I really felt elated. Later when I thought about that "high feeling", I was surprised at myself, after all it was just a driver's license test.

The analysis points at the two parameters: Long expectation (two months or so) and then the surprise. Actually this event was my inspiration for the T/S formula.

Yet, when I received my PhD, an event a bit more significant, I did not experience similar joy. Probably because the ceremony was planned a long time in advance, no surprise there.

It's good to apply this simple understanding to our kids, partners, family, and friends from time to time. It's nice and brings pleasant joy.

To summarize this chapter: it is recommended to recall our moments of joy and elation and to revive them in our memory. It does us good and can serve as a great remedy for "rainy days", which we all experience from time to time.

Chapter 7 – From pleasure to addiction and about money and happiness

The pleasure mechanism in the human brain is similar to that of other mammals. Therefore, it is possible to perform controlled experiments on animals and draw conclusions about us.

The feeling of pleasure is expressed in the brain mainly by the release of dopamine, which conveys the message of reward. This is the same neurotransmitter, known for its role in regulating fine movement.

Neurotransmitters are brain chemicals (molecules), which are released by neurons and serve as some kind of "currency" in the communication between them (i.e. between the neurons).

Only 0.0004% of the neurons in the brain, around 400,000, produce dopamine (dopaminergic neurons). Therefore if some of them perish, the ability to control fine movements may be severely impaired, which occurs in Parkinson Disease patients.

In order to perform efficiently, our brain is able to adjust itself to current conditions and mainly reacts to changes. For example, we become used to the clothes we wear very quickly and most of the time "don't feel" them, except when circumstances change, for example we begin to sweat.

When we drive on a familiar road, the brain usually doesn't react to familiar surroundings and "awakes" only when a change in the usual routine occurs, such as a closed road, an accident or road works. People who live near a noisy street and even people living not far from an airport, manage, in most cases, to sleep well.

The brain knows how to filter "background noise" and not bother our awareness with it.

A similar mechanism causes us not to become "too excited" by a standard level of dopamine.

What happens in the brain when we find ourselves in a pleasant situation, like meeting an old friend, having a good meal or good sex?

In these situations the dopamine level rises and we feel pleasure. Yet, it is possible to abuse this mechanism; the most tragic example is drugs.

In a well-known experiment, rats were trained to push a button in order to receive dopamine. The rats enjoyed the effect of pleasure caused by the dopamine so much, that they became addicted to this artificial pleasure and couldn't stop pushing the button. They didn't care about food or anything else, just continued pushing the button to get more and more dopamine, eventually dying of starvation.

This is a state of addiction.

In the CAGE Test, I discovered that I'm addicted...

CAGE serves mainly to test whether one is addicted to alcohol, but not only.

CAGE comprises of four letters representing four questions, as follows:

1. Have you ever felt you needed to **C**ut down on your drinking?
2. Have people **A**nnoyed you by criticizing your drinking?
3. Have you ever felt **G**uilty about drinking?
4. Have you ever felt you needed a drink first thing in the morning (**E**ye-opener) to steady your nerves or to get rid of a hangover?

I enjoy a glass of red wine with dinner, usually Cabernet Sauvignon or Pinot Noir. On Saturday morning family breakfasts and on other special occasions, I have a single malt whisky. I especially like the 12-year-old Balvenie.

If you reply positively to two out of the four questions above, then you are considered an alcoholic, at least to a certain extent.

I wish to make it clear – although I do enjoy good wine or whisky from time to time, I'm not an alcoholic!

During my stay in India, I haven't even smelled alcohol for three weeks. There was no such possibility... the drinks were mainly ginger water and chai masala, but I really did not miss alcohol.

I have never started a morning with a drink and I really don't feel guilty because of this small pleasure. Regarding "A", yes, indeed, sometimes my family annoys me, but it is only a family joke.

So what am I addicted to?!

When I applied the same test to my habit of regularly checking my email boxes, the result was CAGE 4 out of 4!

Maybe it was understandable when I held senior management positions and received over a hundred emails a day. But now, when I am retired?! It's still the first thing I do in the morning – check my emails. But I try to cure myself.

And when I was in India, although I haven't drunk alcohol, but since there was Wi-Fi available, I checked my emails between meditations...

Is it an addiction? Yes, definitely.

Is it bad?? I don't think so. Many of my friends in hi-tech suffer from the same syndrome, but we all function quite well at work, with the family, contribute to society and live happy lives.

Addiction to money

Studies show that above a certain level, additional money does not contribute to more happiness. One survey found that a yearly salary in the US of $70,000 was satisfactory.

So why do so many wealthy people continue to work hard in order to make more money?! Maybe it's a kind of addiction?!

Or maybe it isn't the money itself but rather the status, a competitive urge, to prove themselves to others.

In many cases, those who seek happiness donate part of their fortune to those who really need it; once they enjoyed making money and at some point they began to enjoy giving to others. Bill Gates, Warren Buffett and Mark Zuckerberg are the most famous, but there are many others.

Summary of this chapter

- ✓ Pleasure is expressed in the brain by the level of dopamine.
- ✓ Experiencing high levels of dopamine may lead to striving to get more dopamine and thus to addiction.
- ✓ Not all addictions are harmful.
- ✓ More money, beyond a certain level, doesn't bring more happiness. It may be meaningful to think about the little money the majority of the world's population lives on.
- ✓ There are rich people who prefer to donate a portion of their wealth than to keep more money in the bank, and maybe this brings them more happiness.

Chapter 8 – Coordinating expectations

Coordinating expectations is one of the most important tools on the way to happiness.

Like bidding in the game of Bridge, one has to set the goals not too low, so the achievement of the objective will have merit, but at the same time not too high, so that it will be achievable. **Advancement toward goals, even if slow, is a great source of positive feelings and happiness.**

Defining goals is an important technique. In a popular "Management by Objectives" a mnemonic acronym – SMART was broadly used once as a guide for setting objectives.

S.M.A.R.T. stands for:

> **S**pecific
> **M**easurable
> **A**mbitious
> **R**ealistic
> **T**ime-bound

The first-known use of the term occurred in the November 1981 issue of "Management Review" by George T. Doran. The principal advantage of SMART objectives is that they are easier to understand and to know when they have been achieved.

Coordinating expectations is relevant to everybody and for almost everything, but the most important is coordinating expectations with ourselves. Failing to meet our own expectations causes frustration and impairs motivation.

When I run on a familiar track, I run faster. This is because I can plan better and balance the effort. My expectations are well coordinated.

But when I try a new track, I'm more careful, run slower, in order to preserve energy for the unexpected. In this case the expectations aren't coordinated and the performance is compromised.

The most important coordination of expectations is with ourselves - what do we expect from ourselves.

A nice and simple experiment is a cold shower. I usually begin with hot water and then gradually turn the knob to colder and colder, then back to hotter and repeat this exercise a few times – excellent for blood circulation.

This works well as long as I regulate the temperature, my expectations are fully coordinated. But, if the water turns suddenly cold, when I am not psychologically prepared...

Another important aspect of expectations is what others (parents, partners, family, friends, bosses etc.) expect of us. Even more important, what do we think about their expectations of us, or how we interpret them.

So the other side of the coin is what we expect of others, which may have a major influence on them. And what message do we convey to them.

A classic example is children and school. If the child thinks or feels, that his parents expect him to be at the top of this class, and he is not, then his self-esteem will be impaired and he will not feel good about himself.

Encouraging to achieve high grades is good and strengthens motivation. But pressure to achieve those highest grades can be harmful. The difference between the two situations can be very subtle.

Another example is the work place, regarding priorities, time or quality. An employee who thinks that he is expected to submit a report ASAP, doesn't check very scrupulously, writes whatever is on his mind at that moment and submits the report on the same day, proud of how fast he was.

But what about the quality?! The boss is disappointed...

If the boss had clearly conveyed the message: "take your time, but do your best", the outcome would have been a win-win. The employee would feel well, knowing that he has done a good job, the boss would be satisfied, compliment the employee, and the employee would go home happy.

Important aspect of coordinating expectations is in eating. Once we decide when to have our next meal, it's much easier not to munch between meals.

If we decide in advance what the meal will consist of, it will be much easier to eat just that. The stomach (brain) will know what to expect and will not "ask" for more.

A good trick is to set a "condition" for the next meal: I'll eat after completing a certain task.

Very important coordination of expectation is in the relations between partners. It may be really crucial for maintaining and enjoying the relationship: will both continue developing their careers?! Maybe he will study first and she will work and later the other way round?!

- When they have children, will she stay at home?! (Will he...?!)
- He is working hard, long hours, and expects that when he comes home, he will be "released" from "house duties"
- She feels that she doesn't get enough help in managing their household
- He expects no interference when watching a football game
- She expects flowers, from time to time.

Obviously, it's good to talk about everything, agree, compromise and **coordinate expectations**. This will definitely contribute to good family relations and happiness.

Coordinating expectations, a mathematical-logical story

A prisoner in the Kingdom of Logic was sentenced to death.

The king decided to fool with him and told him, that "although you will be dead next week, even on your execution day you will be surprised, that this is the day".

The prisoner, who was a well-known mathematician and logician, was very happy.

The execution can't happen on Saturday, because that wouldn't be a surprise!

"But if I'm alive on Friday morning", the prisoner continues his reasoning, "and since it can't be on Saturday, Friday wouldn't be a surprise also!!"

"The same logic applies to Thursday etc. so the king can't surprise me" – declared the prisoner-logician.

Indeed, Sunday and Monday passed peacefully.

But then, on Tuesday, came the hangman, who wasn't skilled in logic, and executed the surprised mathematician...

- ✓ **The most important coordination of expectation is with ourselves.**
- ✓ **The goals shall be SMART.**
- ✓ **Advancement toward our goals, any goals, is a source of positive feelings, it strengthens motivation and contributes to feelings of happiness.**

Chapter 9 – Sub-consciousness and intuition

My sub-consciousness is my best friend and my most efficient assistant.

It works with me long days, overtime and even nights. It probably doesn't need breaks.

When I define a question or a dilemma in the evening, before sleep, the next morning the answers appear by themselves.

I always carry a notebook, because when ideas pop up, it is best to write them down, when they are still fresh and clear.

My explanation for this phenomenon is sub-consciousness.

Maybe a place in the brain free of dealing with the "external world", its noises and interferences.
It's protected, separate and communicates only with the consciousness in its unique way.

I believe that the location of sub-consciousness is in the cerebellum (Latin for the "little brain").

The cerebellum is a major part of the brain, located near the brainstem. It's responsible for a number of functions including motor skills, such as balance, coordination, and posture, as well as eye movement.

It receives information from the sensory system, the spinal cord, and other parts of the brain and then regulates motor movement, resulting in smooth, balanced muscular activity.

Indeed our movements are instinctive most of the time. We do not devote a lot of thought to our next movement or footstep. It is especially evident in the various sport activities.

Beyond the cerebellum's role of controlling motor activities, its other functions are less known, although it is common to assume that the cerebellum is also involved in cognitive functions.

As opposed to the significant advancement in the research of the "big brain", much less is known about the cerebellum, so it can be regarded, to some extent, as somewhat "mystical".

The cerebellum occupies only one seventh of the total space of the brain and this ratio is almost identical in all mammals, which proves that it is quite an old part of the brain.

In spite of its relatively small volume, the cerebellum contains about half of the neurons of the brain, around 50 billion, which makes it a very dense place. Maybe this is one of the reasons research of the cerebellum is so challenging.

Recently a hypothesis has been raised, that the cerebellum plays a role in identifying and dealing with unexpected events. If this hypothesis proves true, it will support the notion of its connection to intuition.

Another hypothesis, which I propose, is that high density and thus the proximity between neurons, contributes to its speed of action. Indeed, all intuitive actions are the fastest, while conscious ones are much slower.

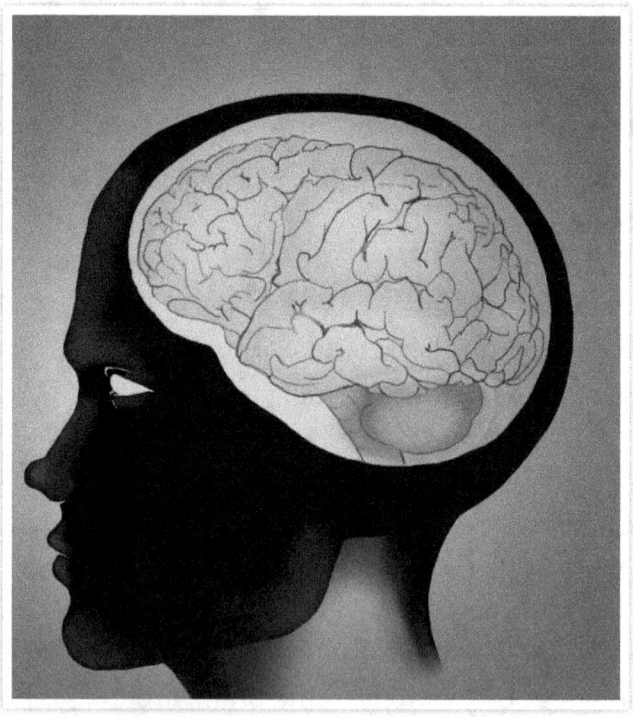

There is a phenomenon which I believe everybody has experienced: we try to recall something, during conversation, and fail. Yet shortly after the conversation ends, it pops right up with no effort.

Making good use of the sub-consciousness and intuition requires training, sometimes many years. It's a gradual process and initially relying on intuition blindly could prove risky. At the beginning it's difficult to identify what is true and right intuition and what is just another thought.

We have to listen, listen very carefully, test what we think is intuition and continuously learn its "voice".

The sign is when we can feel it is right. Feel this is it, this is the right answer and at the same time experience a kind of harmony, agreement.

To reach this level requires training, assigning tasks, missions and questions to the sub-consciousness and testing their outcome.

We probably had those abilities as small kids, but we lost them growing up and living in a complex modern environment. The modern and especially the Western World prefers to rely solely on rational thinking and normative behavior.

I began to restore my relationship with my intuition some 38 years ago, when I started meditating.

Since then, the more I use it, the better the connection has become. Now it's significantly leveraging my abilities.

A good analogy is driving a car. At the beginning it's not easy and we do everything consciously – thinking about everything we do. At this stage any disruption can be dangerous. Our conscious reactions are relatively slow.

And after years of driving?! We don't think about what we do while driving. Everything is instinctive – the sub-consciousness takes over and does a much better job.

I implemented this understanding on my three sons.

All three took their drivers' license lessons when they turned 17. After getting their license they had to have an accompanying driver for their first 10,000 km of driving, which was mostly me.

After they got this experience I knew that they passed the most dangerous stage and have their sub-consciousness to support them. Indeed, all three are very good and careful drivers.

When we hesitate, not sure what's the right thing to do, it's good to "send" the query to the sub-consciousness. And then abandon that specific thought. Switch to something else.

It's important to define the question well, even to write it down clearly on a piece of paper. Sometimes, just devoting thought and effort to clearly define the problem leads to its solution.

The next step is "to release" – this is crucial. As long as we continue to harp on the issue on the conscious level, the sub-consciousness will not "interfere". Try to "forget" and it will come back on its own. Since it's difficult to forget something that is bothering us, the technique is to switch to some other activity.

If the answer doesn't appear immediately or shortly after posing the question, then surely it will arrive the next morning.

And that is the reason for the saying "need to sleep on it".

During my career, there were times, when I had to make dozens of decisions on a daily basis –a truly challenging pace. Although most of the decisions were usually quite routine, there were many significant and not so trivial ones as well.

Experienced mangers know to ask for the relevant data and information, consult and arrive at decisions quite quickly. Those who can't make fast decisions have difficulties to perform well as managers.

But sometimes, even for the best and most experienced managers, some decisions aren't straightforward. In such cases the use of intuition can be very useful. Yet, the decision has to also be carefully examined logically.

A good and experienced manager feels and knows when he makes the right decision.

The sub-consciousness is a great companion!

I call it "my second brain" (but maybe it is the first one?!).

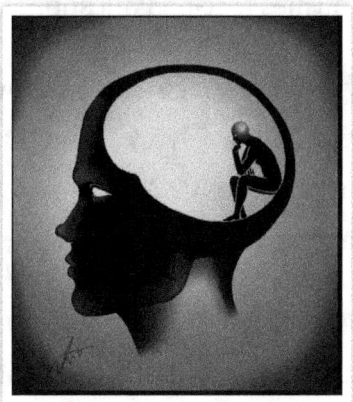

This book was written to a large extend using my sub-consciousness. In the evenings I decided what I wanted to write the next day (a clear definition) and in the morning the ideas and wordings spontaneously appeared in my mind.

Thanks buddy!

"The intuitive mind is a sacred gift and the rational mind is a faithful servant.
We have created a society that honors the servant and has forgotten the gift."

Albert Einstein

Someone asked me once: "how do you communicate with your sub-consciousness?" Good question.

Obviously not with words... if we try to use words, we'll just be talking, talking to ourselves... Well, at least someone listens, nice. But is it useful? Maybe psychologically, the listener always agrees with us.

So how to do it? The sub-consciousness doesn't use words. It does understand words, but answers in its unique way.

The question can and shall be defined by clear wording (with words). But the answer is a sort of guessing. Like in a game, the sub-consciousness will answer only by YES or NO (nodding the head for agreement or disagreement).

As in trying to recall a name. For example: someone tried to recall the name of a US President with the letter "**g**".

I tried to help:

George Bush?! – No.

Gerald Ford?! – No.

And then suddenly it popped up- Rea**g**an...

Another example: a name with the letter "**s**"

Steven?! – No.

Samuel?! – No.

Scott??! – No.

And then surprisingly it popped up, by itself– Mak**s**!

When the right answer appears, we experience a clear feeling, "yes, this is the right answer".

Both cases suggest that the brain doesn't store names alphabetically like a dictionary, according to the first letter. My interpretation – it probably does so according to the most dominant, or the most accented phoneme.

Everybody can find his way to communicate with his sub-consciousness. It may differ from person to person, but for sure it is not language-dependent. **It is a special language of signs.**

A good analogy can be the game "20 questions" – posing any question to the sub-consciousness, in any language, yet it replies only with YES or NO.

The contribution of the sub-consciousness to happiness:
- ✓ **Great help in decision-making processes**
- ✓ **Leverages our abilities**
- ✓ **Provides fast "advice" in fuzzy situations**
- ✓ **Enables us to "go with the flow" and thus be happier**

Chapter 10 – Making Decisions

Every second, millions of neurons "decide" whether **to "fire"** (send a signal) or not.

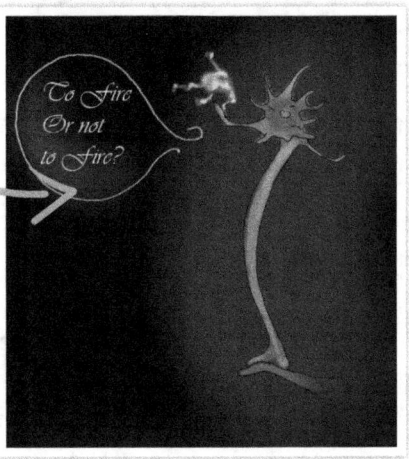

In the famous article: "Maximizing Versus Satisficing: Happiness is a Matter of Choice", Barry Schwartz convincingly claims, that "Satisficers" are happier than "Maximizers".

The term "satisficer" was coined by Nobel Prize Laureate Herbert Simon (1916 – 2001). Simon was an American scientist whose research ranged over many fields, especially cognitive psychology, computer science, economics and sociology, unified by studies of decision-making.

A satisficer is a superposition of two words: satisfy and suffice. It defines a person who is satisfied with a "good enough" decision, meaning, some acceptability threshold is met, vs. a maximizer, who seeks THE best decision.

Satisficers are people who agree with the saying: ***"the enemy of good is better"***. They also make decisions easier and faster. I definitely belong to this category.

Maximizers, seeking the best possible decision, are sometimes caught in lengthy and demanding processes of evaluating all alternatives, all pros and cons. Inherently these processes require time: Gathering all the information, analyzing it and the various potential scenarios, and, after concluding such a process, the circumstances might have changed and one has to repeat the whole procedure from the beginning. Sometimes the information is insufficient, or uncertain, or the optimal solution might be unachievable practically.

For example: A maximizer, while looking for a job, receives a reasonable offer. Being a maximizer, he continues to look for a better one. Meanwhile time passes, he doesn't find the ideal job, comes back to the initial offer, but it's gone, someone else (a satisficer...) took it.

Maximizers can fall into the "Catch 22" cycle: Attempting to maximize their happiness, but failing to achieve the optimum, they become frustrated and consequently less happy.

Another good example is trading stocks.

There was a time when I was quite involved in the stock market and invested in numerous stocks. Two practical rules helped me gain nice profits:

- As a satisficer, I was satisfied with modest gains of 10% - 20% and did not wait for a stock to double its value.

Obviously there were stocks which continued to climb after I sold them with a 20% profit, but these were quite rare and very difficult to predict.

- When a share reached a 10% increase in a month or two, I sold it even with this modest upside.

I know maximizers, who waited for a 100% gain, yet it never happened. BTW, another good rule for trading is *"buy on rumors, sell on news"*.

Making decisions in the Casino

When I played in the casinos in Reno and Las Vegas, I stopped after I won a thousand dollars. This was enough for me at that time.

In most cases if you don't stop in time, you lose everything. One of the secrets of making money in the casino is to know when to stop.

I played Blackjack, a game in which the player has an advantage over the dealer (the casino), if he plays correctly (and the dealer doesn't cheat...)

I won money, mainly due to investing time and effort in developing a strategy, my background in "Games Theory" and Bridge (remembering cards), training, and eventually many hours against the dealer. The key was adjusting the bet, according to the count of cards left in the deck.

If there are more high cards (like king, queen etc.) and less small ones (like 2,3,4 etc.) then the odds are against the dealer. According to the rules he has to draw another card even if he has 16, and thus the probability that he will exceed 21, is high, meaning he will lose.

The higher the ratio between the high cards vs. the low cards, the higher the probability that the player will win, so the bet can be proportionally higher.

Obviously, everything is still probabilistic, but when playing many hands, the Law of Large Numbers prevails.

Law of Large Numbers is a probability theory theorem that describes the result of performing the same experiment many times.

According to that law, the average of the results obtained from a large number of trials should be close to the expected value, and will tend to become closer as more trials are performed.

Since I played hundreds of hands a night, it worked.

Making decisions in games

The same areas in the brain, which are responsible for making decisions in life, are involved in making decisions in games. Therefore, games are an excellent means for simulation and training the brain in making decisions.

In Blackjack, as described earlier, if the player is alone with the dealer, the pace can reach hundreds of hands per hour. For each hand at least three decisions are required: The size of the bet, drawing another card or not (can be more than once) and when to stop. This takes up to an average of at least 300 decisions an hour or on average 12 seconds for a decision.

In the game of Bridge, players are also required to make hundreds of decisions per hour. One game lasts for about seven minutes and is played by four players. So on average a player uses less than two minutes. There are about three to four decisions of bidding, followed by 13 decisions during the game. So the average is eight decisions a minute, or around seven seconds for each decision. This is the average, yet, there are simple, half-automatic decisions which are quicker and others which require up to a full minute.

Chess is different: In tournaments the pace is 40 moves in two hours, which means around three minutes for a decision. But chess is a different type of game – a game with complete information, a game in which everything is "on the table" (in this case on the chessboard). Therefore, the emphasis is on evaluating several possible moves any of which requires an in-depth analysis of what might happen a few moves ahead. This requires time. Computers do extremely well in such games where the number of possibilities, despite being huge, is finite and there are no elements of luck or, more precisely, probability.

As opposed to Chess, Bridge and Blackjack are games with incomplete information, as we do not see the cards of the other players. We can only assume some probabilistic assumptions, or make decisions based on the probability of various scenarios and therefore probability plays an important role in these games.

When I think about my ability as manager to make many decisions quite fast, I believe it probably evolved from the many hours I devoted to competitive Bridge and Chess tournaments.

Nowadays, kids play less Chess or Bridge. However, computer games also require fast decision making, although the characteristics of these decisions are quite different.

It may be interesting to compare the abilities developed in Chess and Bridge vs. the simulation of decisions in computer games.

For satisficers it is much easier to be happy. But to change from a maximizer to a satisficer requires a challenging process, which can succeed only if one is really aware of the need to change, truly wants it and persists. As said earlier, to change a habit takes on average two months and being a maximizer is much more than just a habit.

Satisficers also dwell less on the past. An example is trading on the stock market where there is always a chance of missed opportunities. So what.

As in an old English joke:

"The servant says "my lord, there is a horse in the bath!", "so what" answered the lord"...

My father used to tell me an old wise Russian tale about a boy who lost ten rubles while walking in the forest. The boy started crying loudly. The king of the forest, who heard the crying, suddenly appeared and asked the boy: "why are you crying boy?"

"Because I lost ten rubles", replied the boy.

The king of forest felt sorry for the boy and gave him ten rubles. The boy was very happy.

The king of forest disappeared and after a while the boy, who was a maximizer, begun shedding tears again.

A man passed by and asked the boy: "why are you crying boy?"

The boy told the man how he lost ten rubles and how the king of the forest came and gave him another ten rubles.

"Well, that's nice, so why are you crying again?"

"Because, if I hadn't lost the first ten rubles, now I could have had twenty".

The influence of feelings on decision making

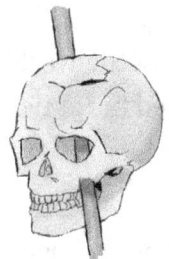

Phineas P. Gage (1823 - 1860) was an American railroad construction foreman. His work involved boring holes deep into outcropping rock; adding blasting powder, a fuse, and sand; then compacting this charge into the hole using a tamping iron.

One day, the iron sparked against the rock and the powder exploded. Rocketing from the hole, the one meter long tamping iron entered the left side of Gage's face passing at the back of his left eye, and out at the top of the head. The iron's tip which entered first was pointed; circumstances to which Gage perhaps owes his life.

Gage was thrown on his back by the explosion, experienced a few convulsive movements of his arms and legs, but remained conscious, spoke after a few minutes and even walked with little assistance.

Gage is remembered for his improbable survival of this accident in which the iron rod was driven completely through his head, destroying much of his brain's left frontal lobe. The injury resulted in changes to his personality and behavior which stayed with him for the remaining twelve years of his life, changes which were so profound that his friends called him "no longer Gage".

Phineas Gage's case influenced 19th century discussion about the mind and brain, in particular the debate on cerebral localization, and was perhaps the first case to suggest that damage to specific parts of the brain might induce specific personality changes.

Another well-known case is the story of Elliot.

In his book, "Descartes' Error: Emotion, Reason and the Human Brain" (first published in 1994) one of the world's top neuroscientists, Antonio Damasio, profiled his patient, Elliott.

Formerly a successful businessman, model father and husband, Elliott suffered from ventromedial frontal lobe damage as a result of a tumor and subsequent surgery for its removal.

Following his operation, Elliot dispassionately reported to Damasio that his life was falling apart. While still in the 97th percentile of IQ, Elliot lacked all motivation. His marriage collapsed as did each new business he started. Damasio found Elliott an "uninvolved spectator" in his own life, "He was always controlled. Nowhere was there a sense of his own suffering, even though he was the protagonist. I never saw a tinge of emotion in my many hours of conversation with him: No sadness, no impatience, no frustration".

It was clear to Damasio that as a result of his surgery, Elliot was incapable of making decisions. "Elliott emerged as a man with a normal intellect who was unable to decide properly, especially when the decision involved personal or social matters." Even small decisions were fraught with endless deliberation: making an appointment took 30 minutes and choosing where to eat lunch took all afternoon. It turned out that Elliott's lack of emotion paralyzed his decision-making.

In the preface to the 2005 edition of "Descartes Error", Damasio wrote, "Today this idea [that emotion assists the reasoning process] does not cause any raised eyebrows. However, while this idea may not raise any eyebrows today among neuroscientists, I believe it's still a surprise to the general public. We're trained to regard emotions as irrational impulses that are likely to lead us astray. When we describe someone as "emotional," it's usually a criticism that suggests that they lack good judgment. And the most logical and intelligent figures in popular culture are those who exert the greatest control over their emotions – or who seem to feel no emotions at all."

Although neuroscience has built a strong body of evidence to demonstrate the inextricable link between reason, emotion and decision-making, most of mainstream culture still doesn't get it.

Management "experts" are still recommending we keep emotion out of decision-making and that professionals leave their feelings at home when they are at work.

The common denominator of Gage and Elliot, was impingement of their emotional aspects in life on one hand, and their difficulties in making decisions on the other.

Regarding Gage, the information is less explicit, as it happened over 160 years ago, but it's reasonable to draw these conclusions, based on what is known.

Looking at their brains, both suffered from a severe damage to the OFC (Orbital Frontal Cortex).

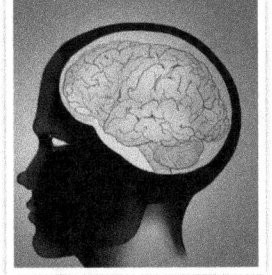

The orbitofrontal cortex is a prefrontal cortex region in the frontal lobes in the brain. It gets its name from its position immediately above the orbits in which the eyes are located.

OFC is involved in the cognitive processing of decision-making and is thought to represent emotion and reward in decision making.

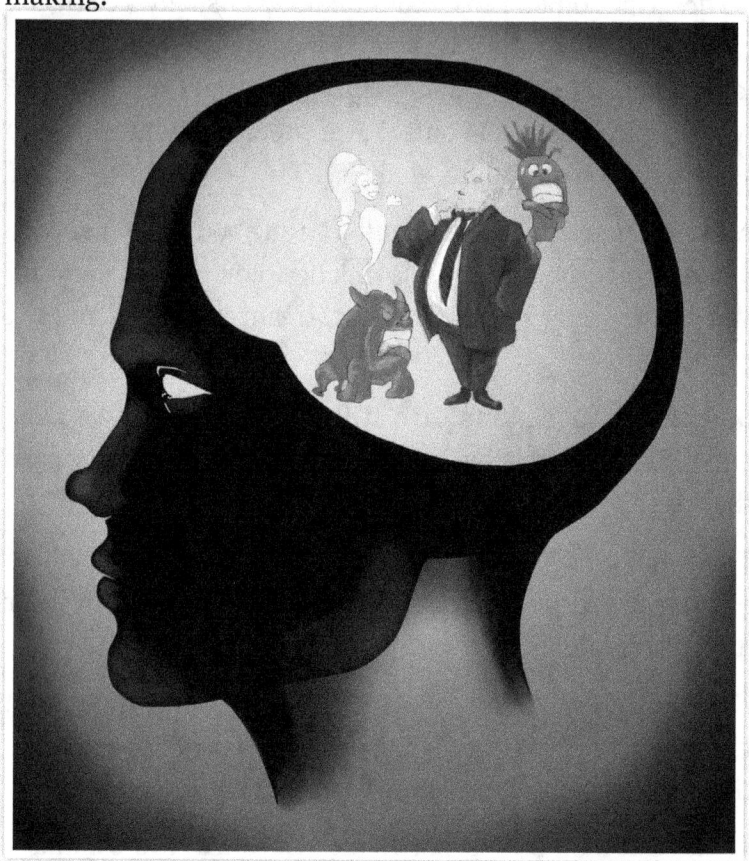

A brain which doesn't experience feelings will have difficulties in making decisions.

What actually happens in a decision making process?

The process comprises of three stages:

- Collecting the information
- Analyzing the alternatives and choosing the best one
- The action – realizing the conclusion of the decision making process

At the stage of collecting information the crucial question is which information is the most relevant and most significant for the specific decision.

Nowadays the amount of information available is extensive, which makes the process of analyzing it all, a "mission impossible".

The simplest example is shopping. Back then there were not so many choices and it was simpler, but today…

Intelligence corps in all armies faces this same challenge, they collect an enormous amount of information, intercept all forms of communication, and then have to seek the needle in the haystack. Another difficulty is the probabilistic nature of the information. The data may be available but what might happen may still remain unpredictable.

Enter the feelings, to assist in preferences and choices similarly to the intuition, as described in the former chapter.

OFC plays a key role in this process, but it's not acting alone: On one hand it's an integral part of the frontal cortex, identified with human intelligence, logic thinking, the ability to draw conclusions, planning, self-control, morality and more.

On the other hand it's interconnected to areas such as amygdalae (singular amygdala), which is involved in many brain functions, including processing memory, decision making and emotional reactions, assigning emotional meaning to external stimuli and marking things as good or bad.

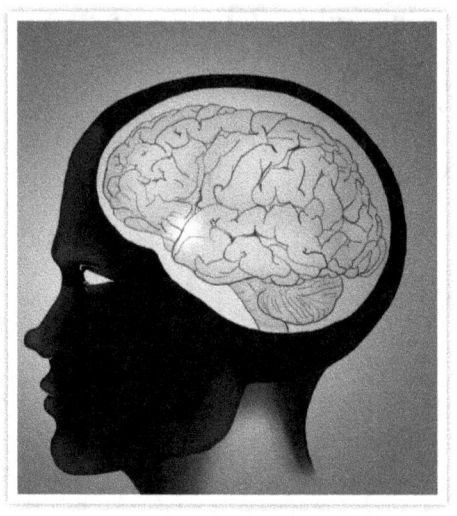

The amygdalae are two small almond-shaped groups of nuclei, located within the temporal lobes of the brain. There are functional differences between the right and left amygdala. Each side holds a specific function in the way we perceive and process emotion.

The right amygdala is associated with negative emotions. It plays a role in the expression of fear and in the processing of fear-inducing stimuli. It also plays a significant role in the retention of episodic memory. Episodic memory consists of the autobiographical aspects of memory. The right amygdala plays a role in the association of time and places with emotional properties.

In contrast, in one study, stimulation of the left amygdala was able to induce either pleasant (happiness) or unpleasant (fear, anxiety, sadness) emotions. Other evidence suggests that the left amygdala plays a role in the brain's reward system.

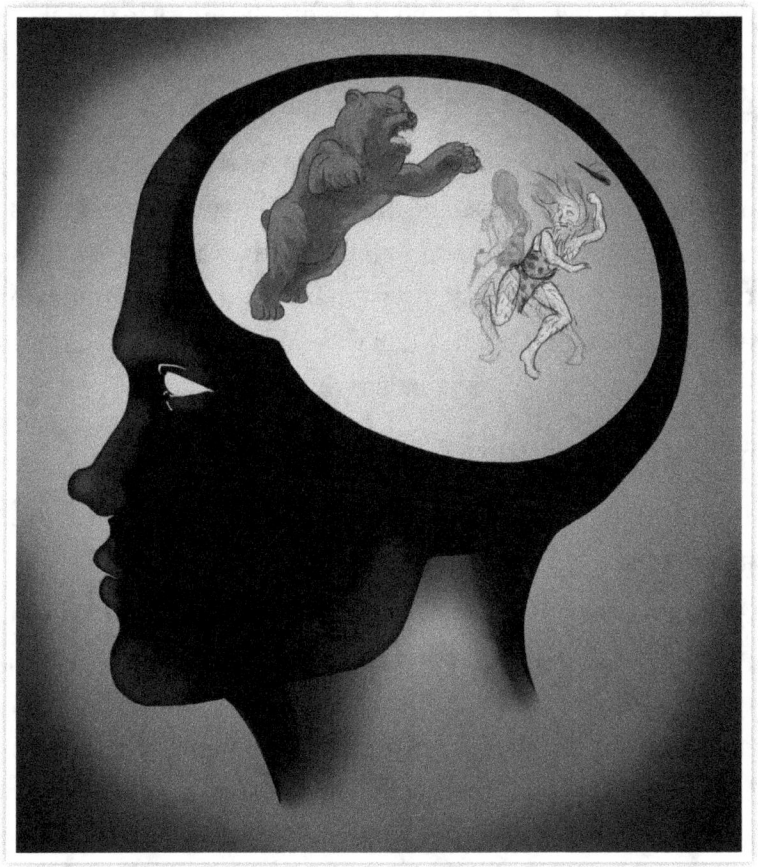

Amygdala – fight or flight

The amygdala learns all these distinctions from our life experiences, but generalizes them and thus is able to mark things as bad or good very quickly, "intuitively".

The hypothesis is that OFC integrates the emotions in the decision making process, and therefore the injury to the OFC, in the cases of Gage and Elliot, caused their problematic behavior and difficulties in making decisions.

This hypothesis fits well the conclusions of the former chapter about sub-consciousness and intuition: The sub-consciousness has already evaluated the various alternatives and has assigned them the positive or negative "mark" and the appropriate emotional "color". Then, when we consciously face the right decision, we feel – "yes, that's right".

The sub-conscious is ahead of us.

It appears that the brain makes decisions before we are aware of it.

Amos Tversky (1937 –1996) was a cognitive and mathematical psychologist, a collaborator of Daniel Kahneman, and a figure in the discovery of systematic human cognitive bias and handling of risk. His early work with Kahneman focused on the psychology of prediction and probability judgment; later they worked together to develop prospect theory, which aims to explain irrational human economic choices and is considered one of the seminal works of behavioral economics. Six years after Tversky's death, Kahneman received the 2002 Nobel Prize in Economics for the work he did in collaboration with Amos Tversky. The prize is not awarded posthumously, but Kahneman told The New York Times in an interview soon after receiving the honor: "I feel it is a joint prize. We were twinned for more than a decade".

In addition to his numerous formal researches, Tversky used to conduct an "informal study" about the decision making processes of his colleagues. One example was making a decision regarding an opportunity to get a position in another city – quite a complex decision. The finding was that even when the initial inclination to the offer was "slightly positive", at the end, in almost all cases it turned to a "fully positive" decision. The brain made the decision before the person was consciously aware of it.

Another example of this phenomenon is the "floating" (undecided) votes in an election. It seems possible to predict a person's vote by showing him relevant photos, and drawing conclusions from his reaction and body language.

Summarizing:
- ✓ **Satisficers are happier than maximizers**
- ✓ **Games are an excellent tool for practicing decision making**
- ✓ **Emotions play a crucial role in making right decisions**
- ✓ **It's OK and recommended to take emotions into account while making decisions**
- ✓ **Relying on emotion, at least to a certain extent, contributes to easier and better decision making, and consequently to happiness**

Chapter 11 – How I got rid of headaches

Pain is a major obstacle on the road to happiness.

In the scope of this book it is impossible to deal with all types of pain. I wish to concentrate on one, or rather a group of pains, headaches. Probably one of the most abundant.

Many of us suffer from headaches which obviously impair our wellbeing and happiness. There are various available treatments, most of which don't usually do a good job.

The positive side to pain is that it reflects the language of our body. Pain is the body's way of warning us that something is wrong or dangerous, for example fire, extreme cold or acid. Much like the sense of taste which enables us to distinguish between bitter, which might indicate poison, and sweet, which is usually a sign of edible food, thus helping us to survive.

Similarly, pain supports physical survival.

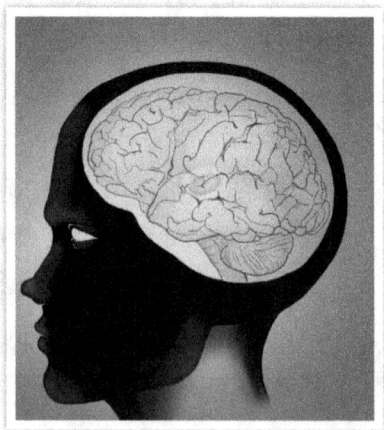

The body utilizes many types of "sensors", each is specific in identifying a different condition – heat, cold, acid and their dangers.

Information from these sensors and from the nerves' tips (all information, not just pain signals), travels through the "cables' transmission" inside the spinal cord, up to the brain where it ends up in the thalamus.

The thalamus (Greek for an internal chamber) is a structure in the center of the brain.

Among its different functions are receiving sensory and motor signals and relaying them to the cerebral cortex. The thalamus also plays an important role in the regulation of consciousness, sleep and alertness.

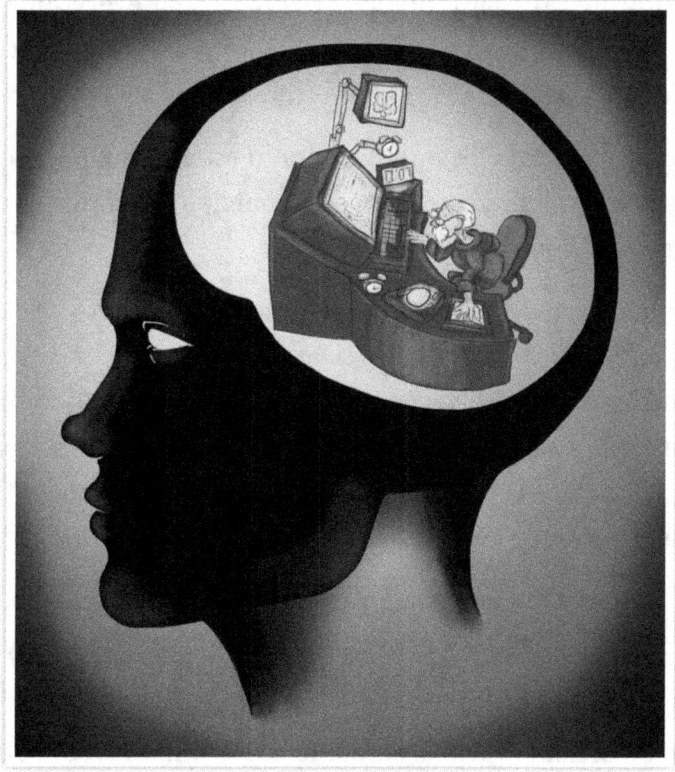

There are more areas in the brain involved in the process of creating the feeling of pain, such as its location (where the signal originated) and even its emotional connection.

The same sensation may be interpreted differently, depending on circumstances. Being hit by someone intentionally may hurt more than an accidental one. A kid will react differently when falling or being hit, when his mother is around than when nobody is there to witness it.

Once, on a cold day in San Francisco, I saw a naked man, sitting in a lotus position with his eye closed, seemingly meditating. At that moment I realized, that everything is actually in our head. We can decide what and how we feel, although it isn't easy, it requires time and practice.

Since then, I have begun to aspire to attain such a level of self-control. I still can't sit naked outside in winter, but I have made some progress.

When I started to look for scientific explanations for this phenomenon, I came across several formal studies. One of them described yogi-masters' unbelievable ability to control their sensations. They did not react at all to sharp pain stimuli, and even their CAT scans did not reveal any signals in the relevant areas in their brain.

Back to the pain signals – these are messages of the body, which we ought to listen to, rather than fight. When we try to surpress the pain, we fight its symptom rather than its cause.

Instead of using various painkillers let's find the root of the problem.

Obviously this is the job of modern medicine. Yet, our subconsciousness can also reveal some truths and as always it's worth listening to it.

Most painkillers block the path of the pain message and consequently, as a side effect, interfere with the normal functioning of the brain. Maybe the pain is alleviated , but our cognitive functioning might be compromised.

Let's recall: **The pain is in the head and in the head only.**

The senses send signals to the brain and the brain may interpret them as pain, but may also interpret them otherwise (like in the case of the yogi masters).

The brain interprets whether it is tickling, fondling or scratching. Yet, even a very gentle touch to an open wound will hurt and the body will shout "don't touch!"

On the other hand we can assign a positive connotation to sensation. For example, I have all my dental treatments (except root canals) with no anesthetization, since I classify the pain as positive and then despite feeling it, it's relatively easy to handle.

I have suffered from headaches for many years, on an average of once a week, usually during or toward weekends. The pain level reached 6-7 on a scale of 0 -10. My interpretation of this timing: The pace of life and work slows down toward the weekend, the level of adrenaline decreases, and the body allows itself to give up.

I tried everything: Putting something cold on my forehead, something hot, cold and hot alternatingly, lying down, sitting up, standing, standing on my head, acupuncture, various pills and painkillers, nothing helped. I guess many of the readers go through a similar experience.

Most of the drugs didn't work at all, some worked for a while, but then the pain returned, even stronger, accompanied by unpleasant side effects. So I stopped taking any drugs and just waited for the pain to pass. It usually lasted between 10-12 hours, occasionally even longer.

I read papers and articles on the subject, some claiming that a solution was found, and others proposing an explanation to the phenomena, but haven't found the remedy.

There are millions of people suffering from headaches and migraines – how come no solution has been found?!

I gave it a lot of thought – thinking logically and systematically, below are the conclusions.

To give you, readers, the motivation to continue reading, here is a "spoiler" – I don't suffer from headaches anymore!

Conclusions:

- There is no one single solution (no "one size fits all")
- Most probably, in most cases, the problem is comprised of several "sub-problems", each with different characteristics. That's why it is so difficult to find THE solution. A cure to one sub-problem may intensify another (the side effects).
- There is a variety of causes. Reactions are unique and differ from one individual to another.
- Therefore, the solution has to be tailored to each one individually and might not be a single one.

- The outbreak of a headache is not immediate. Many causes, such as lack of sleep or tension are **cumulative**. It means that only after the accumulation crosses a threshold, comes the outbreak of the headache. Since it's a process over a time period, the timing of the outbreak can't be precisely predicted, although a repetitive daily routine can lead to headaches on a specific day of the week.

To support the very significant last conclusion, here are two additional arguments:

- On the micro-level, neurons fire after the **accumulation** of enough "motivation" from its neighbor-neurons (enough electric load). Most of the time they don't "fire" – they are not sufficiently "excited"…

- On the macro-level; this is how the **hypothalamus** works

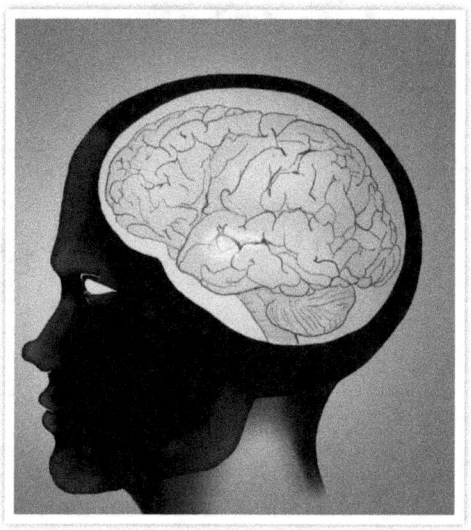

The hypothalamus is a part in the brain, located below the thalamus (hypo = under in Greek), that contains a number of small nuclei with a variety of functions. Among its functions the hypothalamus controls body temperature, hunger, thirst, fatigue, sleep, and the circadian rhythm. There are set points such as 36.6C of body temperature, the CO_2 level, the body acidity level (around pH 7.4) etc. The hypothalamus is responsible for homeostasis – keep each one of these parameters at the set point level, by sending various "commands" to the body, as a reaction to deviations.

Therefore, it is reasonable to assume, that crossing some thresholds may result in the message "***stop***" in the form of a headache.

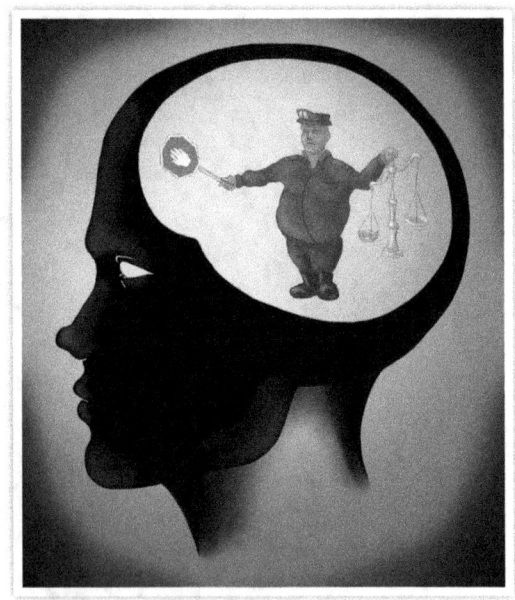

And when we get such a "message, we don't have much choice, we slow down, lie down or stop.

So maybe it is wiser to slow down, before the order from the "cop" – the hypothalamus arrives…

Some seven years ago I started a clinical trial on people, actually on one person – me.

The first "suspect" was coffee, sad.

I loved coffee, especially espresso, and also cappuccino and occasionally even Americano. I tried to stop drinking coffee for a few months and my headaches improved significantly. BTW, each trial has to last for at least a few months. If it is shorter, other confounding factors may interfere. To get a clear picture, we need time.

But I loved coffee... I tried decaffeinated, with cream (to balance the acidity). This helped a little, but the headaches came back more or less as intense as before.

During the trial period I discovered an interesting phenomenon – I didn't have to drink the coffee, just smelling it brought on the same effect! Maybe that is because the smelling sensors are located very close to the brain and therefore have direct connection to it, unlike the drink itself, which has to go through the digestive process, which takes time and can't be felt immediately.

I stopped again. Gave up coffee and moved to various kinds of tea, mainly green and white. The situation improved significantly. There was no doubt, coffee, *for me*, was one of the key triggers of headaches.

It definitely doesn't mean this is true for everybody. Actually there are people who get headaches if they miss their morning coffee. Not surprising, after all coffee is an addiction, a drug, though not a harmful one.

So everybody has to seek his "suspects".

But I do believe that many people may find it relevant for them too.

Although the situation improved, I still got headaches, less frequently and not so strong, but still at least once every two weeks. So coffee was not the only guilty party.

I began thinking what could be the next one. That was easy, the sub-consciousness whispered to me that it was lack of sleep. I had only to verify this hypothesis.

I allowed myself to steal an hour or two from my six-hour nightly budget. When the long working days were not sufficient and I found myself at midnight still answering emails, reviewing reports, presentations etc. I went on until one or two after midnight. My body forgave me for one short night, but when it happened twice or three times in a row, my hypothalamus got angry and punished me with headaches.

So I made a decision - six hours. The compromise can be 15 – 20 minutes but not more. "Good night" at midnight and the alarm clock set to 6AM. It works great and I'm usually up a few minutes before six. The situation improved dramatically. The headaches became even less frequent. But still from time to time they popped back.

The next factor was dairy products. I read about the bad impact of yellow cheese on triggering headaches. I am not sure about that. But the truth is I have considered becoming vegan for a long time, so that probable trigger for headaches was a good excuse.

I believe there was a slight improvement, but barely noticeable, or maybe that's just psychological.

But still headaches happen from time to time.

So I turned to the last suspect - alcohol. I really love good wine or whisky from time to time, so this was a tough one. But, fortunately I found that whisky doesn't harm me in any way. As for wine, it depends on the quantity. A full glass has a negative effect. But half or even a bit more is fine.

Nowadays the headaches have disappeared. It is a great feeling and a real contribution to my happiness.

Of course each one has to seek his personal suspects, as we are different and react differently.

But it's worth a try. Good luck!

Summary

✓ Headache is a message from the body, telling us that we are doing something wrong, or behaving inappropriately.

✓ Headaches are caused by many reasons which differ from one person to another.

✓ It is possible to find the triggers by trial and error, but they should be tested one at a time with enough time allowed for each one.

✓ Since the headaches may not fully disappear following one trial, it is best to write down the occurrences and how strong each one is.

✓ By identifying the causes, we can get rid of headaches naturally, without drugs, and enjoy a better quality of life and thus be happier.

Chapter 12 – Nutrition and Health[2]

How is this related to happiness?!

"Mens sana in corpore sano", usually translated from Latin as **"a healthy mind in a healthy body"**, first coined by the Roman poet Juvenal in the first century CE.

The subject of nutrition is a complex, interesting and crucial for our well-being. Each one of us holds his personal beliefs, which we will not easily change.

Nevertheless, I believe it is worth sharing and presenting some of my personal important understandings. If the reader will devote to them some thought, maybe he or she will find at least some of them useful.

Maimonides already discovered the key role nutrition plays in our well-being and many recent studies support his wise conclusions.

Maimonides (1135 – 1204) was a preeminent medieval Sephardic Jewish philosopher and astronomer and became one of the most prolific and influential Torah scholars and physicians. He believed that bad nutrition is the cause of most malignances.

---

[2] this chapter summarizes my personal experience and things I learned during the years, yet I don't have any formal training in nutrition

His simple but wise recommendations were:
- Eat only when hungry and never become "full"
- Drink only when thirsty

My interpretation of his wise words is that the body will notify us when new supply of food or fluids is required.

We eat because we enjoy eating and because the body needs nutrients. Evolution taught us to enjoy food, consequently ensuring that our body is provided for its needs. It also equipped us with the senses of smell and taste to help us distinguish between what is edible and what can be poisonous, like sweet vs. bitter. With time humans began abusing these good properties of taste and nowadays tend to consume more and more sweets, which induce pleasure. Other condiments and flavors, such as salt or Coca-Cola, deceive our sense of taste and increase our appetite, just because of the pleasure, not because of the need.

Nutrition is a process by which a living organism receives substance and uses it to support its vital activities.

In order to keep and maintain our body in good shape, it is important to balance well between these two factors, enjoying food and providing the body's needs. Quoting Cicero: ***"Eat to live, do not live to eat"***.

To enjoy eating is an easy task, everybody knows what he likes and fulfils this mission quite well.

Regarding the needs, there are three essential food elements: Carbohydrates, proteins and fats, as well as minuscule quantities of all vitamins and minerals, which are crucial for the smooth functioning of the body. The quantities of minerals and vitamins are very small but absolutely necessary.

Carbohydrates - understanding their role and impact is crucial, so let's devote a bit more attention to them.

As the name suggests, they are composed of carbon and water, or on the atomic level: Carbon, oxygen and hydrogen.

There are plenty of carbs in any diet, usually too much of them: Cakes and cookies, potatoes and rice, bakery products, sweets and in nearly every food.

So how much do we need?

Carbohydrates provide most of the energy needed for our daily functioning, both for routine body functions (such as heartbeat, breathing, digestion and brain activity) and for exercise (such as biking, walking, running up the stairs and all types of muscle training). **A humble** supply of carbohydrates is absolutely necessary to sustain a healthy existence but if we don't exercise intensively, we actually need very little: 1 gram of carbs provides 4 calories, so 20 gram is more than enough for a one hour activity. The body keeps reserves for a few days, as 1 gram of fat can turn to 8 calories, so "storage" of a few hundred grams of fat can be sufficient for two - three days of activities. And who doesn't have a few hundred grams of fat, stored for a rainy day... One can fast for a few days and still be able to perform all daily tasks without difficulties.

Carbohydrates are broken down in the body to produce heat and mainly energy. If we run, jog, swim or exercise, we definitely burn calories and use carbohydrates to that end. But still, we don't burn that many of them. Even an intensive half hour of exercising burns only a few hundred calories, equivalent to a nice slice of chocolate cake. BTW, vigorous biking burns the highest number of calories per hour.

If we don't do any significant physical activity, the body doesn't need almost any carbohydrates at all. Just walking, cooking, watching TV and even typing on a keyboard will burn just a few calories.

When talking about using carbohydrates, it's important to mention the other element necessary for producing energy – oxygen. When running becomes difficult, in most cases it is due to lack of a proper supply of oxygen rather than lack of calories. The body creates energy by oxidation, similarly to burning wood in the fireplace. No oxygen, no burning.

While running, we sometimes breathe shallow breathing, thus exchanging only a small portion of the oxygen in our lungs. The solution is to breath out as much as possible so that fresh air will enter the lungs automatically.

Carbohydrates are either simple or complex, based upon their chemical structure. Both types contain four calories per gram, and both are absorbed into the bloodstream as glucose, which is then used to fuel our bodies for normal daily activity and exercise. The main difference between simple and complex carbs is:

- **Simple carbohydrates** or simple sugars - these carbs are fragmented and digested very quickly. Most simple carbs contain refined sugars and very few essential vitamins and minerals. Examples are table sugar, fruit juice, milk, yogurt, honey, molasses, maple syrup and brown sugar.
- **Complex carbohydrates** - complex carbs are packed with fiber, vitamins and minerals and take longer to digest. They are found in vegetables, whole grain breads, oatmeal, legumes, brown rice and whole-wheat pasta.

When we eat (or drink) a simple carbohydrate or a simple sugar – whether it is a scoop of fat-free ice cream, or even a glass of orange juice – all the ingested sugar rushes into our bloodstream quickly, and we feel an immediate boost of energy. Our body then promptly reacts to this sudden spike in blood sugar by calling on the pancreas to produce additional insulin to remove the excess sugar from our blood. For the moment, our blood sugar decreases significantly in reaction to the insulin doing its job, resulting in the need for more fuel, more energy and more calories. And as we hit that residual blood sugar low, we crave more for a quick-release, induced by simple sugars, consequently initiating the sugar craving cycle, the "catch 22".

Complex carbohydrates– are the body's preferred source of energy. When we consume healthy complex carbs – the ones that have not been altered in a food laboratory – they are broken down into glucose molecules which are used as fuel or stored in muscle and in the liver as glycogen. When the body gets even humble supply of glucose fuel and glycogen fuel storage, it can run efficiently. We will then have the energy to function at our best.

When looking for complex carbohydrate food choices to eat, it is best to seek out two subgroups of carbohydrates: Starchy carbohydrates and fibrous ones.

Starchy carbohydrates are found in brown rice, baked and sweet potatoes, oatmeal, brown pastas and whole grains.

Fibrous carbohydrates are found in asparagus, broccoli, cauliflower, onions, mushrooms, spinach and peppers and can also be found in most varieties of dark green leafy vegetables.

Summarizing:

- ✓ **Our body has enough reserves to function without eating for a few days at a time.**
- ✓ **We need very small quantities of carbohydrates, if we are not physically active**
- ✓ **The best carbohydrates, are the complex ones, the starchy and fibrous ones in particular**

Proteins

Proteins are large biomolecules, consisting of one or more long chains of amino acids. We definitely need a constant supply of proteins. The body doesn't store proteins yet needs them on a regular basis for many crucial processes. Proteins perform a vast array of functions within living organisms, including catalyzing metabolic reactions, DNA replication, responding to stimuli, and transporting molecules from one location to another. Each body cell is composed of 20% proteins (65% up to 75% water). Yet, the daily supply of proteins the body needs isn't huge and comes up to an average of 50 grams. For non-vegetarians a single daily portion of meat is sufficient. For vegans, like me, excellent sources of proteins are nuts, almonds and soy products. Proteins are abundant in all natural products, although in relatively small quantities, egg being one of its best sources.

Regarding fats, the body excels in storing them... so we really don't have to worry about a daily supply.

The most important ingredients for the proper functioning of the body are vitamins and minerals.

Vitamins:

A, D, E, and K — dissolve in fat and can be stored in our body. The **water-soluble** vitamins: C and the B-complex vitamins (such as vitamins B6, B12, niacin, riboflavin, and folate), need to dissolve in water before our body can absorb them. Therefore, our body can't store these vitamins so we need a fresh supply of them every day.

B-12 is extremely important. It is crucial in the process of creating DNA, proper functioning of blood cells and participates in many processes in the body.

Lack of B-12 may cause tiredness and some researches claim that it may be one of the causes of neuro-degenerative processes leading to diseases like Alzheimer.

Vegans, like me, lack a natural supply of B-12 and have to take it as a food supplement.

Minerals

The key minerals required by the body are Calcium, Sodium, Chloride, Potassium, Zinc, Phosphorus, Magnesium, Iodine and Iron. There are also a few others, but in significantly smaller quantities.

In a balanced and diversified diet, we usually get the minimal quantities we need of most vitamins and key minerals. In order to achieve that, our daily diet has to include a rich salad and at least one fruit. Many people take the multi-vitamin food supplement to be sure they don't lack any of these important ingredients.

Last, but not least – **how many calories do we need a day?**

It's possible to write down all we eat and count the calories. There are even applications which do it for us. But the truth is that we don't know how many calories we really need a day. The mathematical equation is quite complex with too many unknowns. It's not enough to know our weight, the parameter most commonly used. It depends how much of the weight is fat (doesn't help much in burning calories) and how much is our muscle mass, a key parameter in the metabolic rate, which has the most significant impact on how many calories we burn while resting. The number of calories actually depends on what we have done or plan to do on a specific day.

I propose a simple answer to this complex question, like cutting the Gordian Knot:

> **Not counting calories at all, but weighing ourselves on a daily basis.**

Best in the morning, before cumulating the daily intake of fluids, which at the evening may add a kilogram or more.

If the weight is the same as on the previous day, it means that we ate the exact amount we need. If we gained weight, even a little, let's say 200 grams, it is a warning, which should be taken care of ASAP. 200 grams is easy to lose, but if we do nothing, 200 gram a day can accumulate to three kilograms in two weeks.

The practical solution is to give up something from our standard menu the next day. No need to fast, it may be one slice of bread, or to compromise a little on the desserts which are the best source for "savings". And if you feel a need for a cake or a cookie, there is no need to give it up entirely, just to cut half or even one third off.

Since some of the early readers of this book strongly objected to daily weighing, I looked for scientific support to my recommendation and found the article: "Daily self-weighing within a lifestyle intervention impact on disordered eating symptoms[3]" summarizing an 18-month study with clear conclusions, that daily weighing not only hasn't caused any eating disorders, but on the contrary, contributed to significant weight loss.

Recently, another study was published in the Journal of Obesity: "Frequent Self-Weighing and Visual Feedback for Weight Loss in Overweight Adults"[4] by Carly R. Pacanowski and David A. Levitsky from the University of Minnesota. This study included 162 people (with an average age of 46) who suffered from obesity and wished for ways to lose weight. The researchers set them a goal to decrease their body weight by 10% in one year, a realistic goal. They presented several approaches which could help them, especially making small changes to their dietary habits. For example, giving up dessert a few times a week, smaller lunch and avoiding munching between meals.

The participants were divided into two groups:
- The first consisted of 88 people who were requested to weigh themselves every morning on a standard bathroom scale and record their weight on a website table, especially prepared by the researchers for that purpose.

---

(1) 3   www.ncbi.nlm.nih.gov/pubmed/24245845
(1) 4   hindawi.com/journals/jobe/2015/763680

- The second group consisted of 74 people who were not requested to weigh themselves.

At the end of the study, those who weighed themselves daily lost 2.6 kilograms while the participants of the second group lost only half a kilogram.

In addition, 29% of the members of the first group lost 5% of their weight, while the second group lost only 11%. These results, as well as the outcome of the first study, clearly show the advantage of daily weighing.

An example of a dialog with my sub-consciousness to make a "correction deal": *"Listen my brain, buddy and companion for life. Yesterday we've exaggerated a bit and gained some 300 gram. Although we enjoyed it, which is fine, but 300 yesterday and 300 today after a month our "box" will become a barrel... so tonight we will cut on dessert, instead of two tofu cookies, there will be only one. And no soy-strawberry cream, we skip. Not tonight. Tomorrow we will be back on our regular menu. These dessert budget cuts shall save us 250-300 gram and after all tomorrow will be another day".*

The mass of food

Besides the caloric value of the food we eat, there is also the impact of its volume. When our stomach fills up, a message is sent to the brain and we feel satiated. Therefore the courses' order is important: First drinks or soup, then salad, which also fills the stomach "inexpensively". Some of the salad fibers absorb fluids, swell up and thus fill more of the "free space" in the stomach. Next come proteins, which break-down slowly, and at the end sugars. When we eat in this order, there is a chance that we'll feel satiated and give up dessert altogether.

Eating slowly

The big advantage of eating slowly, the "French Style", is that 20-30 minutes from the first dish, the first satiety signals reach the brain and the strive for more food becomes more balanced.

In a restaurant, if we are not in a hurry, it is better to order each course separately, or at least not order the dessert at the beginning. If we postpone it to the end, the odds that we'll give it up are much higher.

When we go for fast food, we buy the whole meal at once and thus usually more than we need.

Breakfast

The common belief is that a good beginning of the day is with a rich breakfast.

Yet, we just woke up from a long rest and haven't burned a single calorie yet (except if we jog or do any other physical activity first thing in the morning). So, we haven't earned our food yet. As said earlier in this chapter, we do have reserves.

With time, I gave up breakfast and really don't miss it. No hunger pangs in the morning. Around 11 AM my hypothalamus usually sends me the first signals that my body is asking for some refill of the daily supply.

Although breakfast isn't necessary for the energy balance, there is some advantage in using it to awaken the metabolism and raise the metabolic rate. For that end a modest breakfast is enough. It may also be practical, when we do not have time for an early lunch and our next meal will only be in the afternoon.

The big value of eating less

In a well-known experiment on mice, one group was allowed to eat as much as they wanted, a second group was given normal portions and a third group was given half-portions. During the experiment the "eat-all-you-can" mice died first. Those who ate regular quantities lived a normal mice lifespan. Those who ate only half-portions, not only lengthened their lifespans, but some actually doubled the life span expectation for mice.

Summary

- ✓ "Mens sana in corpore sano" - *"a healthy mind in a healthy body"*
- ✓ Eating correctly will determine how we feel during the day and in life in general
- ✓ We have to maintain our body and treat it well, as we'll need its "services" for many more years
- ✓ Food is only a means, not the essence, *"Eat to live, not live to eat"*, Cicero
- ✓ Our ability for self-control, aesthetics and weight loss, for those who wish it, carry a major contribution to how we see ourselves, our self-esteem and happiness
- ✓ "To lengthen thy life, lessen thy meals." Benjamin Franklin

Chapter 13 – An Interlude

It's reasonable to assume that throughout history happy people have always existed.

Nowadays, in many parts of the globe people are happy despite not enjoying the high standard of living of the Western World. They are not aware of Ferrari and are satisfied with a donkey or a yak.

Neither material possessions nor gadgets necessarily determine how happy people are.

People were happy hundreds and thousands of years ago. The feeling of happiness originates in the brain, which evolutionary and physiologically hasn't changed much in the past few thousand years. That isn't long enough in terms of evolution. What did change is the development of the neural network, the synapses, which reflects the richness of stimuli and the contents we have been exposed to in the 21st century.

Despite the fact that the exact biological reaction causing the feeling of happiness isn't known, it's reasonable to assume that, similarly to other feelings, happiness too is a result of a chemical reaction happening in the brain. If this assumption is true, similar reactions most probably occurred in brains of people thousands of years ago.

What caused them to smile, and be happy?! Maybe their family, love or beauty?!

Natural beauty is around us, if we are ready to see it:

- Nature, landscape, flowers, birds, butterflies, animals and people, as well as internal beauty.
- The expression of the beauty of nature in art, first and foremost in painting. Art is very old, and has been with us in its various forms almost from the beginning of human existence. From the walls of caves and up to the golden age of Leonardo Da Vinci and Michelangelo Buonarroti. It's sad that art doesn't receive the acknowledgment and glory it deserves today, in the age of technology and gadgets.

The technology company, which unequivocally values aesthetics and thus in a way integrates technology and art, proved it is a winning formula and became one of the world's leading giants. This is of course Apple.

Steve Jobs always emphasized aesthetics in all Apple products, computers, smartphones and all the others it launches. As a result, people love Apple products and often feel affection to these electronic gadgets.

There is also music, reflecting levels of harmony, which the brain recognizes as good or very good. Melody, beat and harmony are intercepted by the brain through the sense of hearing and bring us pleasure.

Chapter 14 – Family

The term family includes many circles: The nucleus family, siblings, parents, uncles, grandmothers, grandfathers and more. Each circle is significant and can be a subject for sociological and psychological research.

But the most important are the "vertical" relations of parents – children, and the "horizontal" ones, between the partners. There are also parents who are children, for my mum I was a kid, even after I passed fifty.

A separate chapter is devoted to him-her relations later in the book. So, let's concentrate here on children-parents-children relations.

Human beings are unique in nature as children stay dependent on their parents at home for a long time.

Apes also stay together beyond early childhood, but as a herd, a community, rather than as a parents-children nucleus.

Young elephants are left on their own around the age of 12, but most of the other animals don't stay with their parents for long.

The human baby needs long training, maybe because the human brain differs from that of other mammals in the development of its cortex and neocortex in particular.

The neocortex is the largest part of the cerebral cortex in the human brain and is involved in the higher functions, such as sensory perception, decision making, communication, conscious thought and language.

The autonomic nervous system is a control system that acts largely unconsciously and regulates body functions such as heart rate, digestion, respiratory rate, pupillary response, urination, and sexual drive. This system is also the primary mechanism in control of the fight-or-flight response and the freeze-and-dissociate one. Similarly to other mammals, the autonomic nervous system matures quite early, and *if not for the need for the development of the neocortex, human babies could have been "released" on their own quite early.*

In primitive society kids were mainly educated by their parents. In time this process has undergone major evolution. First came the influence of teachers, then friends, and others which replaced the education children received from their parents. In the 20th century the evolution turned into revolution and in the 21th century the Internet, Google and social networks have practically erased the need to learn almost anything from the parents.

These are irreversible processes so "if you can't beat them, join them"...

- ✓ **Parents still play a key role in the crystallization of thinking, opinions, beliefs, values, principles and morals of their children.**
- ✓ **They also have a major influence on the character and self-esteem of the young child, even if neither the parents nor the children admit it.**
- ✓ **They have to adjust their role as parents to fit the 21st Century**

Despite the globalization and social networks, the family is still the most important anchor in our life. Studies show, that one of the key impacts on happiness are the relations of children with their parents. It is not surprising, they were the first to give us encouragement, and to believe in us. So naturally we don't want to disappoint them, and are happy to show them how well we manage and succeed in our life.

I strongly believe that the first feedback we got from our parents stays with us for a lifetime and has a major impact on our self-esteem and self-assurance.

Even when they get older and don't have direct influence on our lives anymore, we still want to share with them the challenges we face, the progress we make and to hear their feedback.

It is important for us how they see us: Winners or losers.

If we receive the trust of our parents at an early age it strengthens our self-assurance and paves the road to success, let's remember that, as parents.

From my early childhood I admired Bobby Fisher.

Robert James "Bobby" Fischer (1943 - 2008) was an American chess Grandmaster and the eleventh World Chess Champion. Many, including myself, consider him the greatest chess player of all times.

In 1972, he won the World Chess Championship beating Boris Spassky of the USSR in a match held in Reykjavík, Iceland, publicized as a Cold War confrontation which attracted more worldwide interest than any chess championship ever. But in 1975, Fischer refused to defend his title and lost it. The 2014 movie "Pawn Sacrifice" allows a glimpse into Fisher's life. It seems that despite his unprecedented achievements he was never happy. Bobby Fisher never met his father. His mother refused to tell him who his father was. I believe that his lacking "half" his parents could have been the major source of his weirdness and unhappy life.

Raising kids

We all believe that we know best, so to dare give advice is risky. Therefore I will refrain from giving advice, but shortly tell how we raised our kids. Judging by the outcome, we have probably done something right.

Below are some of the key principles, which guided us:

- **Explaining ourselves**: Why we do or expect things and certain behaviors
- Dialogues like with **equal partners**
- **Not taking advantage** of parental authority or financial dependence
- **Listening**
- **Fairness**
- **Proportionality** in particular in punishments. For example never a "total no" of TV, but something practical e.g. "no TV for the next three hours", or something similar that we can stand firmly behind and show **consistency**. If we say in a moment of anger: "no more TV", obviously the next day we'll give in, and our **reliability** will be compromised. But three hours, yes, definitely, it's a realistic punishment.
- **Pocket money** for their personal spending – it was theirs, we **never touched** it, so they felt secure about that.
- **Equality** between the brothers. Although there is always an age difference, we adjusted everything according to age, so the younger brothers knew what presents and pocket money to expect, when they reach each age.
- **Coordinating expectations** – *"85 is a very nice grade and good enough in any respect, you definitely don't*

have to chase a 100". As it happened all three did better than that, but this was considered a bonus, not a must. High expectations are good, as they motivate effort, but not too high, which, if not achieved, cause frustration.

They grew up as very close brothers. Once I asked them: "What were the two most significant gifts you got?" (and there were many), the answer was: "My two brothers". The brothers will be with them long after their parents depart to the "next world".

Since this chapter began with cortex and neocortex, let's also mention the neural network. We have some hundred billion neurons from a very early age.

But the connections between the neurons develop as we learn new things and are exposed to more stimuli. The amount and broadness of these connections determine our intellectual abilities.

Therefore we've exposed our sons to a variety of stimuli from a very early age: Chess, playing various instruments, languages. The instruments were available: The first was an electronic keyboard, simple but tempting, then guitars and drums (!), all three loved drums and later piano. Avishai also played the saxophone and clarinet. We didn't push for professional playing, no virtuosity was expected, just to enjoy and get the stimuli.

When they grew up, we played Bridge and even GO. Go (in Chinese 围棋) is a board game involving two players, that originated in ancient China more than 2,500 years ago. It was considered one of the four essential arts of a cultured Chinese scholar in antiquity.

The two players alternately place black and white playing pieces, called "stones", on the vacant intersections ("points") on a board with a 19x19 grid of lines. The aim of the game is to surround an area on the board with one's stones, larger than the opponent's by the end of the game.

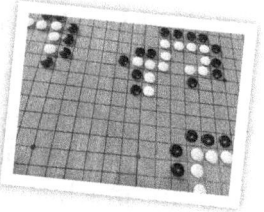

There is significant strategy involved in this game, and because of the size of the board and the number of stones, the number of possible positions is vast and much greater than in Chess! However the rules are quite simple, so it's very easy to teach even a young child.

We also travelled a lot, always the five of us together (the principle of equality). Since my career was very demanding, it didn't leave much time for the family. Therefore the trips abroad were a great opportunity to be together and enjoy family quality time.

From an early age we shared almost everything with the children: Small decisions, big decisions, our financial situation, developments in my career and more. We also listened to them, what was going on in school, with friends, what bothered them etc. We called it **"the principle of information sharing"** (valid until today).

We also shared with them decisions we were facing, for example trips abroad. The next destination was chosen by a democratic vote, each one could propose a destination or two, we compiled a list, and then we voted, anonymously (!) After the destination was chosen, each took upon himself to prepare a plan for one city: to learn about it, suggest the list of attractions, set the itinerary and be our specialist in attendance. Thus, everybody contributed. It wasn't a "parents' trip" in which the parents "took the children along", but rather a joint project.

And we also had our "family shrink"

Ringo *(1995 – 2010)*
was with us almost 15 years
Great friend…

Let's end with a smile, something less serious:

Three successful brothers wanted to impress their old mother. For her 85th birthday, they bought her very special presents.

The first one bought her a large house, the second a Mercedes and hired a driver, and the third bought a unique parrot, which knew the bible, so one could ask him to cite any verse.

And this is what their mother wrote back to them:

John, the house is nice, but too big for me, Most of the time I use only one room and the kitchen. But have to clean all the other rooms too.

Bob, the car is nice, but I'm old, almost don't go out. And the driver is rude.

Jimmy, you know what you mother loves – the chicken was delicious!

Summary

- ✓ The family is still the most important anchor in life.
- ✓ One of the key impacts on happiness is the relations with parents and their feedback.
- ✓ Diversified stimuli, from a very early age, will contribute to the development of the neural network and thus the intellectual capabilities of the children, which will serve them well throughout their life.
- ✓ Children are sometimes challenging, but it is important to look at the greater picture. In the full cycle of life, throughout one's lifetime, children are an inexhaustible source of happiness.
- ✓ Siblings may have different characters, dissimilar temperaments and view things differently. However, a brother or sister has the potential for being the best friend. Even if not on a daily basis, it is good to have a brother or sister in times of need.
- ✓ There is a generation gap. Especially in the 21st century when everything is changing so fast. Nevertheless it is important to remember: we, as children, are the most important for our parents, even if they don't always show it on a daily basis.

Chapter 15 – People

There are many aspects to inter-human relations. In this chapter we'll concentrate on three: **Equality, responsibility and respect.**

Equality

We are all born equal. Although there are genetic differences, the plasticity of the brain enables almost everything. As mentioned in the former chapter, the autonomic nervous system, taking care of all the basic body functions, works from the early days, but the memory is quite "empty" at birth. So it is crucial what will cumulate there during our lifetime.

The family, school, education, friends, and opportunities will shape who we will turn out to be.

Especially how much effort we put, how determined we are and committed to achievements, as well as our dreams and aspirations.

As we are born equal we should always regard others as such.

Responsibility, exceeding beyond ourselves and opportunities

A person being given responsibility changes instantly and the level of his functioning rises dramatically. A good example is soldiers who go through officers training. After graduating the course with the new ranks on their shoulders, and a new responsible and demanding position, they rise above their former level of functioning and usually fulfill the expectations.

When in 2006 I established AMIT (**A**lfred **M**ann **I**nstitute for bio-medical development at **T**echnion), I set the *people* at the top of the list of values of the young organization.

Technion is the Israel Institute of Technology, one of the world's leading technology-oriented universities, located in Haifa.

Indeed, AMIT became highly successful, professional and qualitative with its people feeling good, loving their work place, their colleagues, flourishing and developing: WIN-WIN-WIN.

The main criteria for hiring were personal excelling, motivation and potential. Not necessarily past experience.

Actually what characterized the team was lack of experience. The question one would ask is: "So how did it work?!"

The answer is: by engaging in parallel, professional and experienced consultants and experts on an ad-hoc basis, only as much as needed. The combination worked great, the synergy was very high and the young team learned very fast.

I contributed some coaching, on a daily basis, backing, understanding mistakes, but always expecting to learn from them. The opportunity and responsibility allowed everybody to develop his or her potential, flourish, and at the same time make a major contribution.

I strongly believe that the opportunities we face, or create, and what we do with these opportunities, determine and shape who we are.

"Everything is foreseen, yet free will is granted", a teaching by Rabbi Akiva (40 – 137 CE), a Rabbinic sage, considered by many as the Head of all Sages.

Below are three examples of the opportunities I was given and how the choices I made shaped my life.

- **In 1978 I was offered to join the "RON" project, a joint venture with a US company.** One of the terms was to commit to 9! years of service, three in the US followed by six back in Israel, a long-term commitment. At the time my parents were getting old with only my sister and me to support them. But I saw the opportunity and accepted it with my parents' blessing telling me: "Whatever is good for you". I learned a lot from working with American professionals: How to develop a largescale project, being exposed to a different culture and a much more. And I also got married...

- **In 1992, I got an urgent call from my commander, colonel Reuven Fattal, offering me a mission abroad.** He couldn't elaborate as it was top secret at that time and we were talking over a standard, non-encrypted, telephone line. We were left guessing over the weekend. It appeared that the mission was to serve as the first Israeli military attaché in Eastern Europe, in Warsaw. I hesitated. It was a major deviation from my technological career. Would I succeed? After all I'm a mathematician, not a "classic military man", and Poland?! That country's reputation wasn't good.

- Following our "sharing principle", we discussed it in the family and I accepted. Although there were several candidates, eventually I was chosen and received the nomination. In retrospect it was a great opportunity. The military relations between Poland and Israel back then were at their initial stage, almost non-existing. I started from scratch and had the privilege to contribute to establishing excellent relations between the two countries, lasting until today. Regarding the lack of a broad military background, beyond unit 8200, I actually had some from my service in artillery and of course I learned a lot. So eventually I was able to give lectures (in Polish) to senior officers in the Polish Army and even became friends with the Polish Chief of Staff, Major-General Tadeusz Wilecki.

From right to left: Major-General Tadeusz Wilecki, Major-General Ehud Barak, the Chief of Staff of the Israeli Army, Gen. Wilecki's wife and myself.

At that dinner General Barak said: *"We are three mathematicians around the table"* (meaning himself, Gen. Wilecki's wife and myself). As for the kids, three years in an American school and the exposure to European culture were an experience of a lifetime.

1. **At the end of 2004, I was offered to submit my candidacy to establish the Alfred Mann Institute for bio-medical development at Technion.** Again, hesitations: I was in the midst of a successful career in Comverse, one of the leading technology companies in Israel at that time, while medicine and bio-technology weren't my forte. But again, I saw the fantastic opportunity

to enter the field which I loved and to realize my hidden dreams. The next day (fast decisions...) I submitted my CV. After a lengthy process I was offered the position by the President of Technion. For more than eight years I headed this successful institution, which contributed to the process of commercializing academy-born IP (Intellectual Property), which otherwise would have remained in the academy.

These three junctions had a major impact on my life path, a long and winding road...

The decision to take a one-year leave from the army to write my Ph.D. thesis at the age of 38 wasn't simple also. I was at the climax of my career in 8200 and the risk of failing this almost impossible mission (one year only! for a PhD thesis) was very real. Returning to the army without the degree would have been embarrassing. Yet, I had the feeling (subconsciousness...) that I could do it, but it wasn't based on anything tangible, and one year was a really short time. Once more, in hindsight it appeared to be the right decision. To realize that I had to put enormous efforts, work around the clock with determination, rising above myself.

Respect

I once read a beautiful quotation: ***"Speak only well of people and you need never whisper."*** The wise man who said that was Philip Mogul, a philosopher, a teacher and a physics professor.

I respect and value everybody, whoever he or she is.

I respected Oleg, the cleaning person at AMIT, who in the past served as an officer in the Russian army, yet wasn't ashamed to clean offices. The last time he cleaned my office, he was 80. I listened to him (I learned Russian in school), despite being the CEO and he "just" the cleaner.

When we lived in our first apartment in Netanya, I was already a lieutenant colonel in the IDF. Halil, the Arab gardener from Kalkilyia knocked one day on our door, asking whether he can get some coffee. Since then it has become a ritual. Once a week, on Tuesday morning and wearing my uniform, I served Halil, the Arab gardener from "the territories", coffee with cardamom and cookies on the side, while being a senior officer in the Israeli army, in uniform...

To respect others contributes to their and our happiness.

For example, respecting the people who serve us: In the drugstore, gas station, and restaurant. They work hard and when we treat them nicely, with respect, they feel good.

During my morning jog I meet the early rising street cleaners and always ask them how they are. They answer with a smile, pleasant for them, pleasant for me.

Any technician who comes to our home is treated as a guest: With no pressure and with patience, being first offered coffee or water.

Abraham, the electrician, became almost a family friend and was offered tea, two cups. Abraham believed in fasts, short, medium, long and even ultra-long. He told me about the book

"The Miracle of Fasting", by Paul Bragg, which strengthened my resolve to learn fasting.

The first time I began thinking of fasting was when I read "Siddhartha" by Hermann Hesse. I wrote a note to myself: *"if you can't fast, you are a slave of your stomach"*, but it took me years to achieve this goal. Like any lasting achievement, the process was gradual, evolutionary. I picked Wednesday as the most convenient day of the week (fasting on weekends wouldn't be practical). This is also the day I take a break from physical exercises.

I began with longer and longer intervals between meals, until eventually I reached a 22-24 hour break. Great feeling!

Abraham believed in fasting very strongly. When he was diagnosed with liver cancer, he refused any conventional treatments and only prolonged his fasts. Initially it looked as though it worked: He survived for a few years, fasting and working. The last time he came to fix the electric board, he didn't look well, but was optimistic. Sadly, the next time I called, he did not answer. Later, someone told us that the cancer defeated him, and his fasts.

We tend to judge people by their achievements according to standard measures: making money, succeeding in studies, career, and if someone is good in math, he is considered clever.

But the truth is that we can see and appreciate a variety of skills and properties: Halil could be an excellent gardener, Oleg showed his determination in working hard at the age of 80 and Abraham was an excellent electrician.

Society needs the "outliers" in every discipline and in every profession, not only those in "Outliers - The Story of Success" by Malcolm Gladwell.

I loved the "*quality*" as praised by the American writer and philosopher Robert Pirsig (born 1928) in his great novel *"Zen and the Art of Motorcycle Maintenance"*.

In everything we do, there is a dimension of quality. If we do it well, the quality becomes a value by itself.

Quality doesn't belong only to professors, CEOs or senior managers. It can induce feelings of satisfaction, wholeness and happiness in everybody.

Maya Angelou (1928 – 2014) was an American author, poet, and civil rights activist. I came across her true words:

> "People will forget what you said, people will forget what you did, but **people will never forget how you made them feel.**"

- ✓ Speak only well of people and you need never whisper
- ✓ Everybody deserves to be treated with honor and respect
- ✓ Give credit, kudos, flatter – it is pleasant to others and you will enjoy the reflection of their enjoyment

Chapter 16 – Career and Profession

When I studied mathematics, which actually isn't a profession per se, my father was worried about what I could do with it.

Today perception has changed and there is almost a consensus that mathematicians can be "useful".

Indeed, as a mathematician I succeeded in building a very diversified career, which began at the Department of Statistical Methods in the Central Bureau of Statistics while studying for my MSc, continued with Electronic Intelligence research in the Israeli Intelligence 8200 unit, developing software and algorithms, project management, establishing and heading a department for ELINT Engineering there, serving as a military attaché in Poland, managing R&D, managing investments, serving on boards of Directors in numerous start-ups, establishing an Institute for bio-medical development, founding five start-ups in various fields of medicine and medical devices, stem-cells, and now I'm writing books...

I mentioned Unit 8200. Unit 8200 is the SIGINT (Signal Intelligence) division of Israeli Intelligence. Once it used to be quite secret, but for the past years it is famous for its extraordinary performance, innovation and high quality. Numerous world-class start-ups, some of which grew to be large international enterprises, some acquired by giants, were founded by alumni of that unit. One example is CheckPoint, which invented and brought to the world the firewall.

The book **"Spies, Inc.: Business Innovation from Israel's Masters of Espionage"** written by former TIME magazine and Business 2.0, journalist Stacy Perman, allows a glimpse into what it is all about. Perman writes: *"The most highly successful innovation machine in the world. A little known classified high tech unit in Israeli Intelligence known as 8-200. Its charter is to develop technologies and solutions, customized and suited to the unique challenges of fighting terrorism and endless war."*

Back then I had no idea what I was going to do with math. I simply loved it (the math). With no rational thinking about my future, I followed my heart.

At that time I read "Profession", a short novel by Isaac Asimov (1920 - 1992), an American science fiction author. The story is about education and profession. The author describes a futuristic society, in which children are educated by instantaneous direct computer-brain interface. Members of that futuristic society were taught reading at the age of eight and educated at the age of eighteen. Each one's professional specialty was determined according to an analysis of his or her brain, with no choices allowed on the subject.

George Platen, the protagonist in the story, is determined to become a computer programmer, a profession in demand. But on his "Education Day", he is told that his brain is not suited for any form of education and he is sent to a House for the Feeble Minded.

George stays in the House for a year, but eventually escapes to seek out the doctor who told him he was feeble-minded, and confront him. He arrives at San Francisco and meets a stranger who tells him of different ways to learn, such as reading books and talking with those who already have the desired knowledge.

George begins to understand. He returns to the House and discovers the truth: The House is an Institute of Higher Studies. Those people, who have the urge and persistence to create, even though they have been discouraged about their abilities, are sent there to support the advancement of science and civilization.

Someone has to program the tapes (yes, once there were no DOKs...), that serve the "education".

The lesson of the story suggests that society needs people who are capable of original thought. It is OK to be different and think differently, if you strongly feel that way.

It also conveys the message that **nobody can tell us, what to do and which career is right for us**. This is something that each one has to decide for himself, be sure it is what he or she wants, and then work hard and persist in order to succeed.

- ✓ If one wishes to be happy, choosing the right career is crucial
- ✓ Once we are in, changing our career is a challenge, yet it is possible and may be worth the risk and effort
- ✓ Those who love what they do, have the best odds of being happy

Chapter 17 – Success and luck

"I'm a great believer in luck, and I believe the harder I work, the more I have of it", Thomas Jefferson.

I take Jefferson's words as rather cynical, and interpret them to mean that he essentially believed in hard work.

But luck exists – pure luck. Such as those opportunities happening on our path, and then the question is whether we identify them, and if so, what do we do about it.

Napoleon Bonaparte definitely believed in luck and his saying: *"I have enough experienced generals, but I need those who also have luck"* is famous.

Jefferson lived at the same time as Napoleon, but I doubt whether they met. If they did, they would have probably disagreed …

I believe in the combination of both hard work and luck.

Let's take start-up companies as an example. I served on Boards of Directors of many start-ups and witnessed many which failed as well as those few which succeeded.

The necessary conditions for a start-up to succeed are: Skilled, motivated and passionate entrepreneurs, an original idea, good technology or IP (Intellectual Property) protection as barrier to entry, addressing a large and growing market, the ability to execute, good timing, money, more money, persistence and yes, also luck!

Many good start-ups, despite fulfilling all the above conditions didn't make it. From my personal experience I can mention NetReality, WitCom and RadioTel, in the field of communication, which brought superior products to the market, reached multi-million revenues, but eventually collapsed.

On the other hand is Chromatis, which was acquired by Lucent in 2002 for four billion dollars, a moment before running out of money.

I worked at Comverse Investments at the time and we also managed the ComSor Fund (owned jointly by Comverse and George Soros). ComSor held a small stack in Chromatis, enough to make millions.

But was Chromatis successful, beyond the fantastic EXIT? As far as I know Chromatis' products never reached the market. For Lucent it was a major hit, its shares collapsed and a few years later it merged with Alcatel.

The stars were with Chromatis and the talented, passionate and charismatic entrepreneurs.

A year earlier Cisco bought Cerent, for $7.2B and I remember the wise psychological use of this fact by the entrepreneurs: "we are like Cerrent, but better".

This example demonstrates the combination of hard work, acting right and definitely also luck.

The title of this chapter is "success and luck". Some of the necessary conditions for success were mentioned earlier, but it's important to emphasize persistence. We have to strongly want something, be ready to make sacrifices, define the goals we encounter on our way well, and then be a patient and persistent Marathon runner.

Maybe, if I had met the real Napoleon, I would have convinced him, that the winning combination is both hard work and luck. Maybe he should have put more efforts into coaching his generals...

The photo was taken in August 2002 in Madame Tussaud's museum in London, one month after my last chemotherapy. Since then more than 13 years passed and I'm perfectly well, so how can I say that I'm not lucky.

Here is a short story about luck and what we do with it.

A small bird was flying south before winter. But the weather turned very cold, so the bird froze and fell. It was lucky and fell on a pile of mud, so the fall was relatively soft.

In the mud she began warming up and defreezing. She was so happy, that she started to twitter (not on Twitter...)

A cat passed by, heard the tweeting, pulled the bird out of the mud and ate it.

The moral of the story:
- Sometimes falling on mud can be lucky
- If you are sunk deep in mud, better be quiet
- Not everybody who pulls you out of the mud, is your friend

Summarizing:
- ✓ **If we work hard we may gain more luck**
- ✓ **Pure luck does exist and it's ok to admit it if we get some**
- ✓ **Even if we aren't lucky, we can find something positive in everything**

Chapter 18 – Physical activity

Physical activity greatly contributes to well-being and happiness.

It is also the best means to maintain the body and keep it in shape for years to come. And not only physically: There is evidence that physical activity contributes to the rejuvenation of the brain by some level of neurogenesis ("birth" of new neurons), including in the hippocampus, thus playing a crucial role in creating new memories.

We all have plans to continue our journey on this planet and to this aim we need our body, our mind is not enough.

To maintain our body, we need to provide it with the right fuel, the right nutrition, maintain a reasonable state of mind and definitely also keep it in useful physical condition.

When young, no matter how much we exercise, we can do almost anything, but as we get older, we start to feel the difference in our physical abilities between exercising and not exercising.

Many people are deterred by spending hours in the gym, the entailing costs and time spent.

The message of this chapter is that **a little is a lot.** Studies show that even *5 - 15 minutes of daily exercising at*

home is enough and is effective. 10 minutes are the consensus and who can't spare 10 minutes?!

Once we get used to these small samples and experience the good feeling they induce, we will probably voluntarily expand them a bit more.

The most important point to bear in mind is that **physical exercise should become an integral part of our daily routine for the long run.**

That's why it is so crucial to be practical and do only as much as we can, devoting only as much time as we can afford.

A common mistake is to subscribe to a fitness club, going there three times a week for two hours straight. That's great, but only few can maintain such a strict regime for long.

As **we want something to stay with us for life, the secret is to be practical, and persist.**

Beginning with 10 minutes a day, adding a short jog in the morning once or twice a week, and building an evolving personally adjusted plan over time.

My plan has evolved during the years and today includes jogging and home exercises as the basis. In addition, once a week biking for half an hour, swimming, also for about half an hour, SUP (Stand-up Paddling) and recently I have begun wave surfing. Diversifying the activities makes it less boring and more enjoyable. Once a year I go for one week of skiing.

Overall, it doesn't take more than 3 – 3.5 hours per week and the benefits are worth the "investment" - contributing greatly to my well-being and happiness. There is also some psychology involved. First we have to convince ourselves that it's good for us and worth the effort. Once we are in agreement with ourselves, it becomes much easier to go for it.

Even after we start, there is a psychological aspect to what we do. Even though I have done it for years, before a longer run, or SUP when the waves are higher, I still hesitate, "will I be OK? Will I succeed?" then my best friend (you know him already), my sub-consciousness says: *"look, buddy, you have done it so many times..."*

It's OK to skip a daily exercise once a week from time to time, but not long breaks. If we stop for 2-3 weeks, we have to start all over again. When we go with the inertia, it becomes natural, not asking ourselves too many questions. But after a break, it is much more difficult, so no long breaks!

Rest

The complement of activity is rest; a good sleep, a nap, or meditation. Meditation is addressed in a separate chapter, so let's devote a few words to sleep and shut-eye.

Sleep

Many books address this fascinating subject and I have no intention of competing with them. Below are only a few, but very practical and useful points:

- Preparations for sleep are like landing an airplane: Gradually reducing the activity level, beginning an hour or at least half an hour before retiring.

- Updating the TO DO list: Deleting what we have done and moving what he haven't managed to do to the tomorrow list. The list is important, because otherwise our thoughts would be busy with the chores and plans for tomorrow. Once we write it down, we "handed the responsibility over", after all the piece of paper will not forget…

- Make an effort to fully darken your bedroom: Shutters, lights, even the small LEDs of computers and other devices, otherwise the melatonin (a hormone involved in the synchronization of the circadian rhythms of physiological functions including sleep timing) becomes confused.

- The important purpose of all that is to allow ourselves the right amount of this precious recharger of mind and body. The vast majority of people fall in the range of 6 - 8 hours' sleep, comprising of 4-5 sleep cycles. One cycle usually lasts for 1.5 - 2 hours. It is important to identify what is your personal cycle. It's easiest to wake up at the end of a cycle. Mine is ~90 minutes and I usually wake up refreshed after 6 hours. If one has a cycle of let' say 100 minutes, the best and easiest for him would be to sleep for 400 minutes – 6 hours and 40 minutes.

- Lack of adequate amount of sleep impairs our cognitive functioning and may cause headaches.

Short breaks for the eyes

It's good to just shut your eyes for a moment from time to time during the day, when the input from the visual sense isn't necessary. Just shutting your eyes instantaneously induces alpha waves in the brain and thus some calmness. It also eases the brains' job, as visual information is the vast majority of what it gets from the senses. Even if most of it isn't useful, some level of processing is required, so why not allow the brain some rest when possible. Even when we attend a lecture, it's OK to close the eyes from time to time, and thus improve concentration.

Physical activity and the Alzheimer Disease

It's a well-known fact that the hippocampus, an area in the brain playing a key role in the short term memory (see more in the chapter about learning, later in the book), does not function well in the brain of Alzheimer patients. It is also known, that the hippocampus is sensitive to lack of oxygen.

I'm proposing a hypothesis, claiming that maybe lack of physical activity, less efficient blood circulation and thus less oxygen to the brain, might be among the causes of Alzheimer.

Recent studies show that physical exercise contributes to neurogenesis, in particular in the hippocampus, and thus may be considered as a kind of "preventive maintenance" against neurodegenerative disorders.

It could be interesting to study the correlation between lack of physical activity and this cruel disease.

* * *

I want to share with you a moving song written by our son Nitzan, after the death of my mother. First a few words about her.

Miriam Gilkis was born as Maria Goldberg in Warsaw, Poland. During WWII she escaped with her family to Russia, where she met my father and where my sister Rita was born. After the war she convinced my father to return to Poland where they lived happily for 25 years, and where I was born.

In 1969 we moved to Israel. My mum learned Hebrew very quickly and worked as a bookkeeper for many years. After retiring she learned meditation, as well as keyboard and competitive Bridge. She was even awarded the title of "Silver Master".

Miriam Gilkis

(1924 – 2011)

She was very social and loved by family and friends.

But at the beginning of her eighties, the cruel disease gradually destroyed her impressive cognitive capabilities.

Here is the song. You can hear the touching performance of Shai-Lee Cohen on YouTube:

www.youtube.com/watch?v=vsUWSyC6eTc

 or at the www.HQ100.co.il website or by checking the QR here

Mary

Mary sleeps through most of the day
There is not much she can do anyway
While petals are being picked one by one
All her books stopped making sense, so she pretends she can't see
Conversations are hard, so she laughs constantly
As she wonders how long till what's left is gone

"I'm worthless", she says,
"I'm counting the days"
Tries to hold on to a thought but it slips away
Wipes a tear from her eye, begs "don't remember me this way"

Mary sits and stares at the wall
Can't recall how she got there at all
All the past now just a distant haze
In her hand she clutches a doll
More real to her than the cat, warm and small
Still not grasping why she won't return its gaze

"I'm tired", she said
"Think I'll go to bed"
Now she's speaking but no one can understand
Mary are you still there, somewhere deep inside your head?

* * *

How is this related to happiness?!

Jan Kochanowski, a Polish Renaissance poet, wrote: **"Dear Health, only those who lost you, will appreciate you"**.

We can appreciate it when we wake up in the morning and feel fine, know who we are and don't suffer from any chronic disease. The conclusion: It's worth to invest some effort in physical activity to maintain this precious asset.

Summarizing:

- ✓ The feeling of satisfaction, resulting from physical activity, contributes to happiness.
- ✓ The key is to turn physical activity into a lifelong lasting routine. To achieve that is to be practical, and to appreciate that even short activities are highly valuable.
- ✓ Physical activity not only prolongs life, but also helps to keep its good quality
- ✓ Studies have shown that even moderate activity contributes to neurogenesis, and thus supports maintaining our cognitive abilities

Chapter 19 – Meditation

Meditation is a mental process aimed at attending deeper levels of consciousness.

On November 19th 1977 I received my mantra.

I remember that day very well. I was an officer in the Israeli Intelligence, at that time, a mathematician, with entirely logical and rational thinking. Anything related to soul or mind was very far from me. During that time, I dedicated my evenings to working on my master's thesis in Games Theory, "Repeated Games with Incomplete Information".

After working long and intensive days, I ended up coming home in the evenings quite exhausted, which resulted in very poor and slow progress. I looked for a way to fight these evenings' tiredness and improve my concentration.

A friend told me about a senior officer in our unit who practiced Transcendental Meditation. If it was good for a senior officer, why not for a young lieutenant?

So I subscribed to a course in Transcendental Meditation. It was short, only four meetings, but effective. In the first meeting I received my personal mantra and in the following meetings learned more about the technique of daily practicing.

It worked!

My evening performance improved dramatically.

Yet, the evenings weren't enough for my research so I decided to take a short leave of absence. And I did it! I completed my thesis and received my M.Sc. degree.

Since then, I meditate twice a day, 20 minutes in the morning and about 20 minutes in the afternoon. At first glance it may look "costly", spending almost an hour every day in meditation! But this is definitely a good investment, one of the best I ever made.

Meditation awarded me much more than just getting rid of after-work exhaustion. Every afternoon, after meditation, I feel like a start of a new day. Meditation increases my efficiency. I am able to stay awake as long as I wish. Though I usually retire around midnight to get my six hours of sleep, when necessary I can easily go on until one or two in the morning.

Beyond the practical benefits of meditation, I learned and experienced the fourth state of consciousness: In addition to the waking state, sleep and dreaming – the transcendence.

Reaching beyond thoughts.

The transcendental state is a state where we are aware but have no thoughts.

It is not easy to reach that state without learning a technique. Try it, some thoughts are always there.

When transcending, we stay aware and even though nothing is happening, it is very pleasant, sometimes enjoying moments of great bliss! Initially these moments are quite short, merely seconds, but the more we practice the longer they last.

Today, this state of consciousness stays with me beyond mediation. This is very helpful in life: seeing things clearer, intuition, decision making and a different perspective of life.

Group Meditation is a strong experience. At the end of 2014, toward leaving AMIT, after eight extremely intensive but very pleasant years, I went for three weeks to India.

We stayed on a small campus with people from all over the world, of different nationalities and different beliefs. But all those differences disappeared when we transcended. Together we all reached the same "place", the place beyond thoughts. During the long hours on mattresses, we forgot the body, and the soul went somewhere else…

I believe that practicing meditation of any type contributes tremendously to happiness. I tried several meditation techniques and found the transcendental meditation taught by Maharishi Mahesh Yogi, the most practical and effective. Of course everybody should look for that technique that suits them best.

"The most beautiful thing we can experience is the mysterious. It is the source of all true art and science"
Albert Einstein

The tale of Flatfish

Flatfish were a unique kind of fish. They were two-dimensional, flat, like paper. They lived in a beautiful lake, in a small bay, bordered by a thin strip of wood, which they perceived as impassable. The wood was very thin, only a few millimeters thick, but since they were flat and perceived the world in two dimensions (being unaware of the third dimension, that of depth), they believed it to be a real barrier.

One day, a very creative fish was enlightened, discovering the third dimension it shouted "Eureka!", dived and crossed the barrier.

We owe the fourth dimension of time-space to Albert Einstein, in addition to the three which are intuitive to everybody.

In mathematics it is possible to define more dimensions. Theoretically there is actually no limit, and there can be an infinitive number of dimensions.

Maybe one day, another Einstein, or an exceptionally creative flatfish, will discover another dimension and we will be able to cross the barrier and reach a beautiful infinitive lake of freedom.

By meditating, I discovered the fourth state of consciousness and I'm aware now that there are more: Cosmic Consciousness, God Consciousness and Unity Consciousness. Maybe one day I'll enjoy experiencing the next level of consciousness.

Summarizing:
- ✓ Meditation opens a window to a new dimension in life
- ✓ It is an effective technique to get rid of some of the tensions and stress we all cumulate in our daily life.
- ✓ It is a major factor on the path to happiness

Chapter 20 – "Stop Worrying and Start Living"

A common perception holds that our life comprises of three time periods: Past, present and future.

But **real life** actually happens only in the present.

It is highly important to understand this simple truth. The past we carry on our shoulders during our lifetime is often a heavy load and a hurdle on our path to happiness. Sometimes it is the unknown future, and sometimes both.

But the past doesn't actually exist anymore (we can't go "Back to the Future"...), it is gone and will not return.

And the future is on the horizon, or beyond it.

People waste time and precious vital energy dwelling on their past (which in any case can't be changed), or worrying about the future.

Both are reasonable to some extent. We all have pleasant memories which are nice to relive from time to time.

As for the future, we definitely have to plan it, even if not all our plans will eventually be realized. Yet, worrying about all potential future disasters doesn't help much. Most of them will never happen, while the worries do influence our feelings and behavior.

How do we free ourselves of thinking about our past misfortunes and the unknown and sometimes unpredictable future?!

Let's take an analogy from the world of chess. In a given chess board position, the player has on average 35 potential moves he can make. If he plans the next move, the number of possibilities totals 35x35, namely, about 1000. If he plans three moves ahead it reaches over 30,000 possibilities.

Obviously nobody can evaluate 30,000 potential situations. Even a chess master can't do that. But he does evaluate at least three steps ahead, usually even 6 – 7, or more.

So how does he do it?!

The grand master knows from his chess experience what are the 3 – 4 most relevant moves in a given chessboard position. So he analyses only these few possibilities in depth.

The same is relevant to life: we know from our experience which two – three scenarios are the most likely to happen in a given life-situation (life is simpler than chess in the number of potential moves…).

Yet, you might ask: "what about all the other, less probable developments". Right, everything is possible. But even the chess grand-master cannot consider all possible moves, he would go mad.

If we worry about all the "less-than-one-percent" possibilities, we are wasting our time, impede our life-performance while unable to protect ourselves from everything anyway. Some people "buy" this kind of "insurance" by trusting their fate to the "hands of God".

The practical solution is to play the "Game of Life", take the risks and not worry about everything that may or may not happen.

I'm sure this understanding is shared by many, although not necessarily implemented even by those who do understand it.

Dale Carnegie (1888 – 1955) was a writer and a guru of techniques for self-development and success. In his book: ***"Stop Worrying and Start Living"***, the same as the title of this chapter, he addresses the issue of worrying very practically.

I hope I'll not offend him, by summarizing his book in two sentences and an example:

The first principle: **Accept the situation.**

The second principle: **Do the best to improve the outcome**

The most picturesque example I remember from the book is a case of a man, who was told that he has an incurable disease and has six months left to live. He went to a Dale Carnegie course (these were very lucrative courses at that time) and implemented the first principle – accepting the fact that he is going to die in six months. Then, according to the second principle, he bought a coffin (to be "ready") and went on a journey around the world.

During his great journey he forgot about his illness and Death forgot about him, as he lived for many more years, happy and worry-free.

A very similar message was proposed by a contemporary of Dale Carnegie, the Indian mystic and sage, who moved to the West, Meher Baba (1894 – 1969), in his expression:

"Don't worry, be happy"

In his lectures Baba preached, similarly to Dale Carnegie – *"**do your best, but if you haven't achieved all you wanted, don't be frustrated**"*.

In 1988, Bobby McFerrin noticed a poster with these four words and inspired by the expression's charm and simplicity, wrote the now famous song.

Can fit well as an anthem for this book...

The Dalai Lama said once about man:

Man sacrifices his health in order to make money. Then he sacrifices money to recuperate his health. And then he is so anxious about the future that he does not enjoy the present; the result being that he does not live in the present or the future; he lives as if he is never going to die, and then dies having never really lived."

Summarizing:
- ✓ **Accept the situation**
- ✓ **Do your best to improve it**
- ✓ **Do the maximum, but not more. Don't be frustrated, if you haven't achieved all you wished for**

Chapter 21 – Learning

Learning was the key motive for my PhD thesis.

Although it also contains mathematical theorems and complex formulas, its essence is learning processes.

My inspiration stemmed from the marvelous performance of the human brain, while still being quite a slow machine. The brain is actually slower by orders of magnitude than any basic PC. You can compare your performance by multiplying two five-digit numbers.

So what is its secret?!

The answer is memory.

This claim might raise an eyebrow. After all, the computer "remembers" everything we put into it, while we can barely remember a small fraction. For example, if we compare what we remember from a one-hour driving, we come up with very little. The GoPro camera will remember everything.

Or, when we sit in a restaurant and see people at a table nearby, if we bump into them a month later we would most probably not recognize any of them. But if we store a photo on a disk, no problem, the image is saved for ever.

Here comes the beauty and the power of the human brain. We'll remember the scene very vaguely, but with all the information we may need for any practical purpose.

The key term I proposed was ***stochastic patterns***.

Patterns - we remember scenes in the form of patterns. Similar to a restaurant behavioral model: waiting to be seated, sitting at the table, the waiters, the people, the menu, the food, the drinks, enjoyment and the check. Another example is, the familiar way home. We do not actually keep many details in our memory. We know the rough picture and the context is very helpful. But if someone shows us a photo, a close-up of the tree we pass by every day, there is no guarantee that we will recognize it as that one which bids us hello every morning.

Stochastic - probabilistic. Let's explain, using an example of by-passing a car in front of us, on a single lane road. If a computer will have to do it (and Google is pursuing this futuristic luxury), it would have to first collect all the relevant information: The distance between us and the car in front of us, the distance from the car coming from the opposite direction, the speed of all three cars, the ability to accelerate etc. [Maybe I shall offer Google my PhD thesis]. But people don't do that!

Millions of drivers by-pass cars every day and in most cases successfully.

So how do we do it?!

Very simply, by using stochastic patterns!

We cumulate the experience of all our past by-passing, so we are able to roughly estimate that if the distance is so and so, the speed is so and so and we are driving a classic Mustang, we will probably succeed. Drivers do err and that's why accidents happen. A well programmed computer is supposed to do it perfectly, once it received all the relevant data.

As above said, we build the patterns based on our experience,

but what about the first time, when we have no previous experience. Right, that's tough. Recalling the first time we drove a car (if one can recall...), it was a challenge.

Why is it difficult to recall? It is the same as the difficulty to remember whether we locked the door when we left the house.

It all boils down to these patterns. Similar scenes are merged into one stochastic pattern and are not remembered as individual instances. This is also the storage efficiency of the human brain!

The human brain doesn't perform any computations, it only compares a certain pattern to the stochastic one stored in our memory.

So what's **the claim to fame** of my PhD thesis?

I translated these intuitive processes into a mathematical model, theorems and formulas, which provided answers such as: How many examples does the system need in order to perform on a specific level (i.e., 100 for 80% success, 1,000 for 95% etc.) and what should be the quality of the examples.

One of the intuitive, but nice conclusions was that **the most efficient is to learn from good examples.** The better the examples, the better and faster the learning.

A common lesson claims that we should "learn from mistakes". Well, that's true too and it is good to complement learning from good examples with learning from mistakes (preferably of others…). But this is slow and costly learning. Each mistake may carry a "cost", so if one makes too many mistakes…

The effect of learning from good examples, leading to better and better performances, can be seen in many disciplines. It's clearly evident in chess, as the best games are easily available for studying and indeed a world champion from the 20s of the 20th century would have a tough time competing in a contemporary tournament.

The same goes for other sport disciplines (yes, chess is a sport, even though we don't use the whole body…).

It can be seen as an evolution of human intellectual and other capabilities.

Beyond math, I also demonstrated the model on the game of chess. My PC received a book of examples of French Defense openings for dinner.

It digested it through the night and in the morning, despite the all-night effort, was refreshed and was able to pass a test on the most relevant moves in specific French Defense examples (which it has not seen before).

I implemented the theory on our three sons. After receiving their drivers' license, each one had to drive 10,000 km either with me or with one of the older brothers, to gain experience, before being left on their own. The outcome was very good and the three turned out to be very good drivers.

Examining the brain, the physical process there is expressed by richness of the **neural network**.

From early childhood our brain contains about 100 billion neurons.

There is still a myth that we are losing neurons on a daily basis. If you heard that myth and are worried about your cognitive performance deteriorating over the years, I'm happy to assure you that it is just a myth. We can maintain our cognitive abilities as long as we use them, are physically active and supply the body (and brain!) with the right nutrition.

That myth originated from a study in the fifties, when human brains, analyzed post-mortem, were found to be significantly smaller. The researchers concluded that the brain shrinks over the years and thus the theory. The research sample of that study was brains of people who died of neuro-degenerative diseases. The researchers unjustly generalized the conclusion to healthy ones.

As for the neural network, as said, the number of neurons is pretty stable throughout our lifetime. Yet, the neural network is continuously developing. New synapses (Greek for conjunctions) are created and existing ones are strengthened, as we learn new things and are exposed to new stimuli.

A synapse is a junction where signals are transferred from one neuron to another. It can be seen as an evolutionary "re-wiring" of the brain connections, resulting from experiences and stimuli. Obviously each single event has only a miniscule impact. The number of synaptic connections varies significantly from person to person and ranges between a hundred trillion up to a thousand trillion!

The quality of this connectivity has a direct impact on our associative thinking and cognitive performance in general. An analogy is a "well-connected" person, who can achieve more in life.

We've implemented these understandings on our kids. They were exposed to numerous stimuli from a very early age: Playing various musical instruments, chess, bridge, GO, languages and more.

Nitzan, six months old, on a chessboard...

Indeed all three have succeeded extremely well in school and in their higher education studies.

Not only children can learn, but we as adults are capable of learning throughout our lifetime.

I definitely personally implement it in learning new things which is one of my greatest pleasures. I am very fond of "The Great Courses" by the Teaching Company. They have the best teachers and I took their courses studying biology, medicine, brain, neuro-science, quantum physics and much more. Coursera courses are great and the Internet provides an infinite supply of knowledge in any field.

Learning new things is the best anti-aging therapy, it makes us feel younger, induces a feeling of elation and thus contributes to our happiness.

The role of the hippocampus

The learning process in the brain is based on memory. No memory – no learning. In this context it's important to mention the hippocampus (named for its resemblance to a seahorse (hippos - horse and kampos - sea monster, in Greek) which is a major component in the brain of humans and other vertebrates.

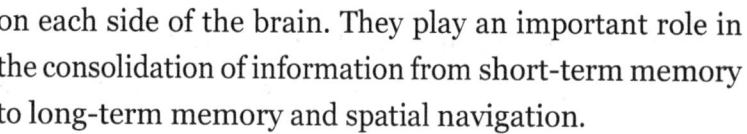

Humans and other mammals have two hippocampi, one on each side of the brain. They play an important role in the consolidation of information from short-term memory to long-term memory and spatial navigation.

The hippocampus and some adjacent areas in the medial temporal lobe are crucial in the ability to acquire and store new memories of facts and events we experience. This is the declarative memory comprising of the "what" type of information, as opposed to the explicit memory, storing the "how" (for example knowing how to ride a bike).

In addition to converting short-term memory into long-term memory and storing it, the hippocampus also plays a key role in retrieving long term memories.

All the information from the senses passes through the hippocampus which serves as a kind of "switchboard".

An example which demonstrated the key role of the

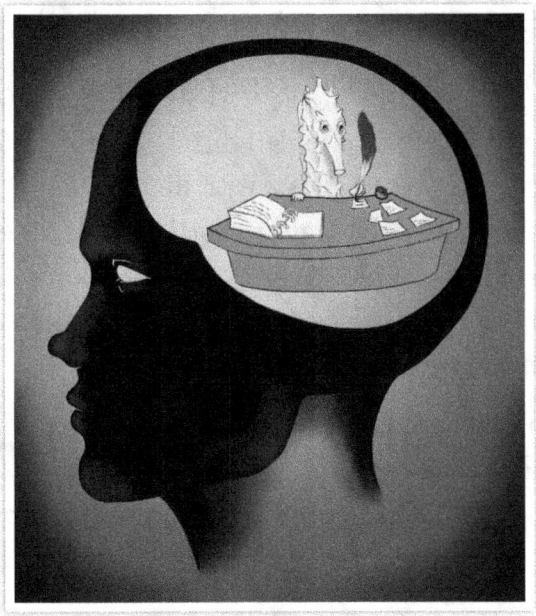

hippocampus in creating new memories was the case of Henry Gustav Molaison (1926 – 2008), known widely as H.M.

Molaison was an American who suffered from a memory disorder. He underwent surgery in which two thirds of his hippocampi was removed, in an attempt to cure his epilepsy. The operation was successful in almost totally curing his epilepsy, but resulted in unexpected side effects.

The key change following the surgery was the total loss of Molaison's ability to form new memories, an ability which as a result of this case was understood to be associated with the hippocampus. The case played a very important role in the development of theories that explain the link between brain function and memory.

As opposed to the cases of Elliot and Gage, Molaison remained a nice person, although a bit confused and embarrassed.

The 2000 film "Mememto" thrillingly reflects this condition.

Molaison was widely studied during his long life. One of the researchers who worked with him for many years was the Canadian neuropsychologist Brenda Milner, who is considered as the founder of neuropsychology. She met Molaison numerous times and each time he repeated politely: "My name is Henry, nice to meet you"...

We think about ourselves in the language of our memories: Childhood, adolescence, life experience, life stories etc. Henry Molaison lost his memory and actually didn't know who he was.

Summarizing:
- ✓ **Learning from good examples is much more effective than learning from mistakes, although learning from mistakes can complement the good examples.**
- ✓ **If we stop learning, we will be left behind.**
- ✓ **Learning new things brings joy and elation.**
- ✓ **Learning is based on memory. No memory – no learning.**
- ✓ **We are who we are due to our memory.**

Chapter 22 – Between her and him

This chapter is dedicated to all young couples, but not only to the young ones.

The key understanding is very simple:

Don't take him or her for granted!

As the saying goes: "There was great love, but then they got married..."

Marriage is the longest contract we ever sign, but with terms which were set centuries ago. Not sure they fit the 21st Century's reality that well, and the high percentage of divorce is sad proof that the model is probably not ideal.

But once we enter this agreement, the most important thing is to maintain it well, invest the effort, be creative, persistent **and allow for compromises.**

The first principle is listening: Understanding what really matters, knowing what is really important for your partner increases the odds to succeed in the relationship multifold.

The second principle is breaking the routine: Finding the time (remember the big stones?!) to go out. Not just to a restaurant, this is easy, and does not necessarily contribute to a better relationship (maybe contributes to some unnecessary calories...).

I believe that going dancing is the best way of spending time together as a couple.

In the classic movie "Zorba the Greek", when everything collapses, Basil and Zorba walk on the beach frustrated and disappointed and the tension is high. Then, suddenly, Basil, dressed in his white suit and tie, as fit for an English gentleman, turns to Zorba and asks:
"Teach me to dance!"

They begin dancing the Sirtaki step by step, which evolves spontaneously.

They enjoy the dance, begin laughing and the tension fades away. Maybe they even feel some happiness.

Not only dancing, time-out in nature, a trip, even a challenging one. A flower from time to time, not as a routine, just as a small token to show that you care or on a nice day, when you feel happy just to share.

Each couple should find the model that suits them.

It is hard to believe that the ancient formula is a "one-size-fits-all" solution.

The high percentage of divorce is the sad proof that the formula isn't perfect, so it is worth finding adjustments.

How are relationships reflected in the brain?

According to Hellen Fisher from Rutgers University, there are **three stages involved in a relationship: Desire, attraction and bonding.**

At the **desire stage** the leading factors are the hormones: Testosterone in men and estrogen in women.

I believe that on the strategic level, people have to be ready and want to fall in love.

I propose a hypothesis: Most true falling in love phenomenon happens at a relatively young age, the twenties and even teens.

Yet, there is a cultural shift, due to the significantly longer life span. The "preparation stage"- academic studies, developing professional career and seeking some economic basis, takes longer and consequently the 'ready stage' of falling in love happens at a later age which results in a catch 22 – seeking love when being "too mature".

The 'being in love' stage idealizes the partner, seeing mainly his/her good qualities and being blind to their weaknesses.

The more mature we are, the more difficult it is to see the positive balance of virtues and vices of the partner.

* * *

How we fall in love, the first meeting

A psychological study found three key factors as influencing the outcome of the first meeting:

Body language – 55%

The intonation of our voice and the way we talk – 38%

The content, what we say – only 7%!

All this happens during the first 90 seconds up to a few minutes of the first meeting. That's it. Our impression is fixed and it will be very difficult to change it.

It's therefore better to save your efforts as it will be never the same as "love at first sight".

The attraction stage

At the attraction stage the main players are adrenaline, dopamine and serotonin:

Adrenaline: When in love, we react like we do in stress situations. When meeting the loved one, our heart beats faster, we may feel dryness in the mouth and even sweat.

Dopamine: High levels of dopamine were found in the brains of young couples in love. Dopamine conveys desire, pleasure and reward. The effect in the brain resembles that of cocaine.

Serotonin: High levels of serotonin, similar to that of OCD (Obsessive Compulsive Disorder), explain the constant thinking about the loved one.

The stage of bonding and strengthening the connection

At this stage the key player is oxytocin, commonly called the "love hormone" or the "bonding hormone", which is produced mainly by the hypothalamus. Oxytocin is associated with strengthening the connection between the partners and also between parents and children, in particular between the mother and her newborn baby, especially when breast-feeding. The hypothesis is that the process continues as the baby grows up, and expands to include the father, when he is involved in raising the baby.

Most of the research on oxytocin was done on rats, although evidence was found in humans too. It shows that during sex and especially during orgasm, large amounts of oxytocin are released (yes, some people were willing to do this for the sake of science, while letting the researchers peek into their brains).

High levels of oxytocin were observed also in the brains of couples in a deep romantic love. These high levels were preserved throughout the study which lasted, unfortunately, for only six months. At the same time intensive activity was also observed in those areas of the brain dealing with reward and addiction. Maybe evolutionarily, love can be regarded as the first addiction.

The long term

It appears that as time passes the levels of dopamine and adrenaline decrease. Fisher believes that oxytocin has a negative impact on them. Maybe this could account for the reason why "crazy love" usually doesn't last very long.

Gradually "blindness" disappears and we are able to see the imperfections of our partner.

If in the meantime the oxytocin levels rise sufficiently, the bonding is firmed and relations last.

A study in Texas University shows, that one of the factors in building strong and lasting relations is long courting. The longer the courting, the better the relations thereafter.

Maybe "hard to get" is the right tactic...

The study mentioned earlier emphasizes the impact of body language and voice intonation in the first meeting.

I would like to propose an additional factor: a deep direct gaze into the eyes of the partner. Eye to eye, which is actually brain to brain. The eye is the only organ directly connected to the brain with the sight nerve going directly from the retina to the brain, therefore looking into one's eyes is like looking into his brain.

So the correct saying should be not from heart to heart, but rather from brain to brain...

As an anecdote, a recent study found high levels of oxytocin in dog owners. The levels were especially high while the dog was gazing at his master's eyes.

Summarizing

- ✓ Don't take your partner for granted.
- ✓ Dancing will contribute more to the relationship than going out for dinner.
- ✓ It is necessary to invest in maintaining the relationship. A flower from time to time.
- ✓ There are advantages in falling in love at a young age (there are disadvantages too…).
- ✓ Long courting may contribute to stronger and lasting relations.
- ✓ If you have a partner, sex and thus more oxytocin, may also contribute to strengthening the bonding.

As in any kind of relationship, there are always ups and downs. When reaching a "down time", it is important to remember all the highs reached together and envision future pinnacles.

Chapter 23 - A short love story

Love is one of the key aspects of the relations between her and him. It is a huge subject and more was written about love than about any other subject.

Below is a beautiful song written by our talented son Nitzan. You can hear the original and subtle performance of Liat Ben-David at the www.hq100.co.il website, on YouTube www.youtube.com/watch?v=jkioGAGFHO4 or by checking the QR here.

So Beautiful

I never knew love could cut like a knife
Until the day you came into my life

It took me by surprise
Your heavenly brown eyes
Your smile that shines like morning sun
Conquered my heart and soul
Love I could not control
I knew my life has just begun

Tell me why you had to be so beautiful
Why did we have to meet, why did I have to fall
I try to tell myself to move on

That I'm better off on my own
Why did you have to be so beautiful

I know that we were never meant to be
But my heart is locked and I can't find the key

My love for you is blind
Can't get you off my mind
Although I know there is no hope
No matter how I try
This love I can't deny
Will this torture ever stop?

Tell me why you had to be so beautiful
Why did we have to meet, why did I have to fall
I try to tell myself to move on
That I'm better off on my own
Why did you have to be so beautiful

Chapter 24 - Getting older: Dreams, wishes, aspirations and "The Bucket List"

- ✓ We can measure age by the number of times Earth revolved around the Sun
- ✓ If we want better resolution, we can count the number of sunrises.
- ✓ It's also possible to measure lifespan by the number of breaths we'll breathe. By this measure, if we breathe slower we'll live longer, and see more sunrises...

I heard a theory once, that the faster an animal breathes, the shorter its life expectation (dogs breathe fast). But I haven't studied this theory in depth.

It's also possible to see the passing years as a process of growth and development, and like the aging of wine leading to better quality.

But wine ages in high quality barrels and the longer we want to keep it in the cellar, the better the conditions have to be in order to preserve its quality.

The same goes for humans, and several thoughts were raised and discussed throughout the chapters of this book: the right nutrition, physical activity, rest, some spirituality, peace of mind and more.

It is also possible to measure age, as proposed by Shimon Peres, the ninth President of Israel, at the opening of the BrainTech conference in Tel Aviv, on March 11th 2015, at the age of 91: "The bigger the dreams and aspirations a person has, the younger he is!"

Assume for a moment that you lost your personal documents: ID, driver's license etc. and also lost a small fraction of your memory – forgetting your birth date. How will you know how old you are?

I propose **measuring age according to how long we have left to live, to stay on our beautiful planet**. Obviously we don't know, but mathematically it is a valid statement.

* * *

And maybe the day we'll know is not far?!

By measuring telomeres we can know the theoretical limit of replication of cells in our body. A telomere (in Greek telos - end and meros - part) is a region located at each end of a chromosome, which protects its end from deterioration or from fusion with neighboring chromosomes.

Empirical evidence shows that the telomeres associated with each cell's DNA will slightly shorten with each new cell division until they reach a critical length making further cell division impossible.

In 2009 Elizabeth Blackburn, Carol Greider, and Jack Szostak were awarded the Nobel Prize in Physiology or Medicine for the discovery of the way chromosomes are protected by telomeres and the enzyme telomerase.

The estimations are that there are between 50 and 75 trillion cells in the body. Each type of cell has its own life span. Red blood cells live for about four months, some white blood cells live very shortly but most live for more than a year. Skin cells live about two or three weeks. Colon cells die after about four days. Sperm cells have a life span of about three days, while brain cells typically last an entire lifetime.

As for heart cells the estimations are that no more than half are replaced during our lifetime.

Most cell types replicate themselves to replace dying cells. Yet, there is a limit to the number of times a normal human cell population divides until cell division stops and the population enters a senescence phase. This aging of the cell population appears to correlate with the overall physical aging of the human body. The concept was advanced by

American anatomist Leonard Hayflick at Wistar Institute in Philadelphia, Pennsylvania and is known as the Hayflick limit.

Blackburn, Greider, and Szostak also discovered the role of reactivation in cell "immortalization" of the enzyme telomerase.

Maybe in 2029 other scientists will win the Nobel Prize for a "telomerase longevity drink" which will prolong the telomeres and thus the potential life expectation.

But there is a catch, if we live too long and not die naturally, maybe we all will get cancer sooner or later. It is possible that evolution 'invented' telomere shortening not necessary to limit human's lifespan but maybe to protect us from getting cancer by limiting the number of cell divisions.

Another path to immortality is stem cells – "naïve cells" which can evolve into almost any cell type. They can divide infinitely in their stem cells state, and therefore can be considered as a storehouse of materials to repair body organs.

In November 2012 I was among the founders of Accellta, a stem cells start-up, and headed it for over two years since then. I truly believe that stem cells will become one day the real personal medicine, allowing the replacement of cells, tissues and organs in the human body.

***

It is natural and good to dream and have aspirations. Not everyone succeeds in fulfilling all of his/her dreams and wishes. Most of us realize them only partially, but dreaming and aspiring is an important aspect of life. It inspires creativity, strengthens motivation, and boosts energy. Many times dreams actually come true.

* * *

I belong to the admirers of Steve Jobs for his way, creativity, wisdom and contribution. Below is a short citation of one of his wise sayings:

Your time is limited, so don't waste it living someone else's life. Don't be trapped by dogma - which is living with the results of other people's thinking. Don't let the noise of others' opinions drown out your own inner voice. And most important, have the courage to follow your heart and intuition.
Steve Jobs

The beautiful quote below is attributed to Benjamin Franklin:
"We don't stop playing because we grow old; we grow old because we stop playing."

Summary:

- ✓ We can see the passing of time as a process of development and like the aging of wine leading to better quality.
- ✓ Having dreams keeps as young. Place the big stones in "The Bucket List" and begin realizing them.
- ✓ Our time is limited, let's not waste it on living the lives of others.

Chapter 25 – Time, and reversing aging

We live in a four-dimensional space-time. Space-time is a model in physics that combines space and time into a single interwoven continuum. The space-time of our universe is usually interpreted as consisting of three dimensions (length, width, height) with time as the fourth dimension. Dimensions are independent components of a coordinate grid needed to locate a point in a certain defined space.

For example, latitude and longitude are two independent coordinates on the globe which together uniquely determine a certain location. In space-time, a coordinate grid that includes the 3+1 dimensions, locates **events (rather than just points in space)**, namely, time is added as another dimension to the coordinate grid. In this way the coordinates specify **where and when events occur**.

If we want to meet someone, we have to agree on the place (the three geographic coordinates), but also on the time, otherwise we will arrive at the meeting point at different times and miss one another.

The first one who proposed this four-dimensional space-time was the German mathematician Hermann Minkowski (1864 – 1909). Minkowski is best known for his work on relativity, in which he showed in 1907 that his former student Albert

Einstein's special theory of relativity (1905), could be understood geometrically as a theory of four-dimensional space–time, since then known in physics as the "Minkowski space-time". Yet, most people associate this model with the student rather than the teacher...

Time is the only dimension in physics having one direction only – **"the arrow of time"**. In the three-dimensional space we can move back and forth, left and right, up and down, but back in time, not yet. We can pick a point in space and get there. But we can't select a point in time and reach it (at least not now), maybe that day will come, like in the movie "Back to the future", or like the case of Benjamin Button.

In the meantime we can look back on our timeline on Facebook.

In terms of formal physics: It's impossible to turn the time arrow backwards, because time is measured by entropy (a measure of "disorder") which, according to the second law of thermodynamics, never decreases.

simple examples are a scrambled egg, which cannot be turned back into a whole egg, or the milk we add to our coffee.

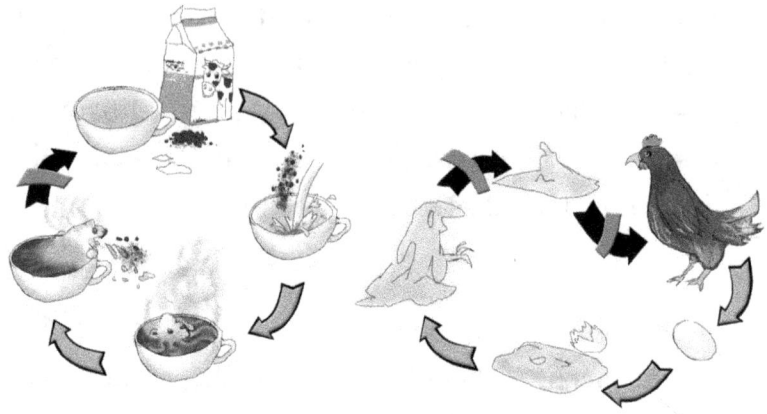

There are those who adopt the approach that as the past is gone and the future is unknown both are therefore meaningless, therefore, we should live only in the present.

I believe this goes too far: Our present and future are built on the past. Moreover, we do know quite a lot about the future, the simplest example is the weather forecast which is predictable for a week or two ahead.

We also know, with high probability, where we will be tomorrow and the day after. Of course nothing is full-proof, yet a lot depends on us ("everything is foreseen, yet free will is granted"). Making plans is foreseeing our future which we ourselves determine.

In his book "A Brief History of Time" Stephen Hawking wrote: "The increase of disorder or entropy is what distinguishes the past from the future, giving a direction to time."

Once I got a fortune cookie with the following sentence:

A lost pinch of gold may be found. A lost pinch of time, never.

Very true. And that's why time is such a precious resource

We receive a precious gift every new day – 86,400 seconds, to use during the day and we should appreciate every moment.

Sometimes even one second can make a difference. For instance being involved in a car accident or avoiding it. And there are situations, when even a fraction of a second makes a difference, such as Olympic runs or swimming finals.

So let's give some respect to THE TIME.

When I was hospitalized after surgery to remove the tumor, I rented a small TV. The pains were still strong and I didn't have the patience to watch any news, so I watched the "Nature" channel, maybe it was "National Geographic". An Indian in the show asked: **"The white man talks a lot about time. What is time? I asked them to *show me the time*..."**

Years later, I found that a similar question was asked some 1700 years ago by Aurelius Augustinus (354 – 430), also known as St. Augustine, an early Christian theologian and philosopher whose writings influenced the development of Western Christianity and Western philosophy. Augustinus is cited as saying: "What is time? If I'm not asked, I know. But if I have to explain it to someone, I wouldn't know".

* * *

"The Last Question" is a science-fiction novel by Isaac Asimov. The story deals with the development of a universe-scale computer called Multivac and its relationships with humanity. In the fifties, such a super-computer was definitely science-fiction, but today Google and the Internet are not far from being "omnipotent" or at least "knowing everything".

Each time a different character presents the computer with the same question; namely, how can the death threat to human existence and the universe posed by heat, be averted. The question was: "How can the net amount of entropy of the universe be massively decreased?" This is equivalent to asking: "Can the workings of the second law of thermodynamics be reversed?"

Multivac's only response after lengthy "thinking" is:

"INSUFFICIENT DATA FOR MEANINGFUL ANSWER."

The story jumps forward in time into later eras of human and scientific development. In each of these eras someone decides to ask the ultimate "last question" regarding the reversal and decrease of entropy. Each time, in each new era, Multivac's descendant is asked the same question, and finds itself unable to solve the problem. Each time all it can answer is:

"THERE IS AS YET INSUFFICIENT DATA FOR A MEANINGFUL ANSWER."

In the last scene, the god-like descendant of humanity watches the stars flicker out, one by one, as matter and energy ends, and with it, space and time. Humanity asks AC, Multivac's ultimate descendant, which exists in hyperspace beyond the bounds of gravity or time, the entropy question one last time, before the last of humanity disappears. AC is still unable to answer, but continues to ponder the question even after space and time cease to exist.

Eventually AC discovers the answer, but has nobody to report it to; the universe is already dead. It therefore decides to answer by demonstration. The story ends with AC's pronouncement:

"LET THERE BE LIGHT!"

And there was light...

The story makes it apparent that the time's arrow question could be considered beyond science, as philosophical or even religious – and there was light.

Time is precious. According to the law of "supply and demand" it's priceless, as it can't be bought. Yet, in order to be happy, we need time, the more the better.

What's the solution?!

Not to waste it. A common example is our devoting time to the news. It is natural, curiosity is a strong drive. There are even applications for constantly feeding us real-time news.

Is it really useful?! Helpful?!

How many times have the news really affected our daily life?

Maybe the weather does, but it can be checked on any smartphone instantaneously.

* * *

The rabbit in Alice in Wonderland is always in a hurry: "I'm late, I'm late"…

What message did the author, who was also a mathematician and a philosopher, want to convey to us?

Maybe that we, the people of the modern age, have lost some of the joy of life, because we are always in a hurry?

* * *

Instead of the standard units of time: years, months, days, hours and seconds, derived from the movement of Earth, I propose a new "currency", maybe better reflecting our life experience.

The currency of events:

The more events occur, the more time passes.

If nothing happens, like on the Hawaiian beach, the time is not passing

With no events –time stops…

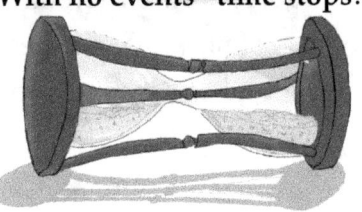

Reversing aging?!

Following the earlier discussion on the challenge to turn the Arrow of Time and its relation to entropy, we know that the Arrow of Time could be turned in the opposite direction only if we can decrease entropy.

I would like to propose a ***"personal reverse of time"***, namely **reversing aging.**

Maybe we can decrease the entropy in our life, by slowing down and reducing the pace?!

- ✓ **We don't always have to fill every free moment with plans.**
- ✓ **Make less commitments**
- ✓ **Leave some free time, unplanned just to enjoy the moment, whatever it is.**

Until recently, my life has been extremely intensive; the more I advanced in my career, with studying at the same time (formally and informally), and spending time with family and friends, the more hectic it grew.

Since I retired a year ago, I have been devoting time to writing, more studying and lots of physical activities, trying to slow down, slightly. Indeed, and as a result, my overall feeling is great and I feel younger.

So maybe it works...

Time summary

✓ A lost pinch of gold can be found, a lost pinch of time, never.

✓ Time is the most precious resource; it's priceless, because it can't be bought.

✓ The modern man is losing some of his joy of life, because of being always in a hurry.

✓ Does watching or listening to the news really contribute to our daily life and wellbeing?

✓ It's possible to measure time by events, the more events and experiences we have the longer our real life is.

It takes a long time to grow young.

Pablo Picasso

Chapter 26 - About me

I was born in Poland and came to Israel at the age of 17. Arriving in Israel I joined a kibbutz, where I learned Hebrew and worked in a grapefruit orchard.

Later on, I went for an undergraduate degrees in Mathematics, Statistics and Computer Science at the Hebrew University of Jerusalem. Continuing my studies I earned my MSc in Mathematics with a thesis on Games Theory. At the age of 40 I went back to school for my PhD, in Management Information Systems with a thesis on Artificial Intelligence.

I served for more than 17 years in the 8200 SIGINT Unit of the Israeli Intelligence.

In 1992, I was awarded the highest "Award for Israeli National Security" projects by the President of Israel.

Artist view of the project on the Golan Heights.

My last appointment during my military career was as the first military attaché of Israel in Poland and Hungary. During that time I had the honor to meet on several occasions Yitzchak Rabin, the Prime Minister of Israel at that time, whom I admired very much.

Returning back to Israel I retired as colonel and started my second career.

From 1995 - 2006 I held senior positions in Comverse Technology (S&P 500 Co. at that time). Initially I headed the R&D of the Audiodisk Division (now Verint, Nasdaq VRNT) and later on, for over eight years, managed investments and served as director in numerous start-up companies.

In 2006 I accepted the offer by the President of Technion to establish and head "AMIT" (Alfred Mann Institute for Biomedical Development).

An essential part of the Institute was the establishment of five start-up companies in various fields of medicine, medical devices and stem cells, which I conducted and served as an active chairman in all five.

I'm a proud father of three sons, whom I raised together with Carmela. Nitzan got his BSc in Computer Science and his MSc in Information Sciences, Avishai earned his MSc in Physics and is currently studying toward his PhD in Astrophysics, and Omri is an architect, but following his heart and dreams is pursuing the world of animated movies.

We travelled abroad a lot, visiting all in all over 30 countries, always the five of us, as long as the boys could and wanted to come.

On the Pacaya volcano in Guatemala, the last trip together, September 2010. From left to right: Nitzan, Avishai, Carmela, Zeev and Omri.

In 2013 Nitzan got married to Basmat and the family expanded. In January 2015 we were blessed with our first granddaughter Kinneret.

Chapter 27 - Coda

If you are reading this page, and hopefully have not skipped too many chapters, maybe you are somewhat happier already. If not, a bit of patience, it will come.

It's reasonable to assume, that the readers of this book are among those who seek better understanding of life and self-introspection. Therefore, the beautiful quote from Herman Hesses's Siddharta, may be relevant.

"It's true, I'm old," spoke Govinda, "but I haven't stopped searching. Never will I stop searching, this seems to be my destiny. You too, so it seems to me, have been searching. Would you like to tell me something, oh honorable one?"

Quoth Siddhartha: "What should I possibly have to tell you, oh venerable one? Perhaps that you're searching far too much? That in all that searching, you don't find the time for finding?"

www.ingramcontent.com/pod-product-compliance
Lightning Source LLC
LaVergne TN
LVHW022232080526
838199LV00105B/242
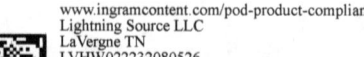